OVER-THINKING ABOUT YOU

Navigating Romantic Relationships When You Have Anxiety, OCD, and/or Depression

ALLISON RASKIN

WORKMAN PUBLISHING · NEW YORK

Library of Congress Cataloging-in-Publication Data

Names: Raskin, Allison, author.
Title: Overthinking about you: navigating romantic relationships when you have anxiety, OCD, and/or depression / Allison Raskin.
Identifiers: LCCN 2021030972 | ISBN 9781523513222 (paperback) | ISBN 9781523513222 (ebook)
Subjects: LCSH: Dating (Social customs)—Psychological aspects. | Interpersonal relations—Psychological aspects. | Man-woman relationships—Psychological aspects. | Mentally ill—Social conditions. | Mental illness—Social aspects.
Classification: LCC HQ801.R257 2022 | DDC 306.7—dc23
LC record available at https://lccn.loc.gov/2021030972

ISBN 978-1-5235-1322-2

Design by Sarah Smith

Workman books are available at special discounts when purchased in bulk for premiums and sales promotions as well as for fundraising or educational use. Special editions or book excerpts can also be created to specification. For details, contact the Special Sales Director at specialmarkets@workman.com.

Workman Publishing Co., Inc.
225 Varick Street
New York, NY 10014-4381

workman.com

WORKMAN is a registered trademark of Workman Publishing Co., Inc.

Printed in the United States of America on responsibly sourced paper
First printing March 2022

10 9 8 7 6 5 4 3 2 1

To my sister, Jocelyn, who has been there for every single breakup and will one day stand next to me at my wedding

This book is a blend of memoir and self-help. It relies on my memory as well as my interpretation of events— both of which are most likely skewed in some way as a result of being human. Many names have been changed throughout to respect people's privacy.

———————

Contents

Note to the Reader

Before we dive in, I'd like to acknowledge that I am writing this book from the perspective of a white, straight, cis woman. While I have struggled with my mental health for almost my entire life, I have done so from a place of extreme privilege. In addition to familial support, I have also had physical and financial access to the best treatment available. This is not the case for many people, and it would be disingenuous of me to imply otherwise.

The sad reality is that the majority of clinical psychology—including the research the field is built upon—is geared toward white westerners. Although many strides have been taken in recent years to include a multicultural approach to counseling, there is still a lot of work needed to repair the relationship between the mental health field and marginalized clientele. People from marginalized groups are also less likely to receive care due to cultural, racial, and socioeconomic disparities. So while I encourage the use of professional mental health services throughout this book, I also want to recognize and validate why some of you might be reluctant or unable to do so.

It's equally important to acknowledge that the intersection of mental health and dating is often more complex if you are part of the LGBTQIA+ community. According to the National Alliance on Mental Illness (NAMI), "LGB adults are more than twice as likely as heterosexual adults to experience a mental health condition. Transgender individuals are nearly four times as likely as cisgender individuals to experience a mental health condition." These statistics are heartbreaking and show the damaging effects of marginalization and disenfranchisement. I am not able to speak to these added complexities personally, nor would I attempt to, but I use masculine, feminine, and gender-neutral pronouns throughout in the hope that everyone will be able to see themselves in these pages. While I recognize that I have limited personal experience, my goal is for this book to be as inclusive as possible.

Lastly, this book discusses suicidal ideation, self-harm, fat-antagonism, and weight loss and gain. Trigger warnings will be provided at the beginning of each chapter when needed. Please read responsibly (and with a lot of self-love).

Resources

For those located in the United States, check out the following resources for more information.

Inclusive Therapists

inclusivetherapists.com

A mental health network that centers the needs of Black, Indigenous, and People of Color (BIPOC) and the 2SLGBTQIA+ community; offers resources; and helps pair clients with therapists who are the right cultural fit.

National Queer and Trans Therapists of Color Network

nqttcn.com

A healing justice organization that aims to increase access to social justice-oriented mental health services by helping queer and trans people of color (QTPoC) locate QTPoC mental health practitioners across the country.

Therapy for Black Girls

therapyforblackgirls.com

An online space dedicated to encouraging the mental wellness of Black women and girls.

The Trevor Project

thetrevorproject.org
Call 1-866-488-7386

A national 24-hour, toll-free confidential suicide hotline for LGBTQIA+ youth.

The LGBT National Help Center

glbtnationalhelpcenter.org

Provides free and confidential peer support for people in the LGBTQIA+ community through hotlines, chat rooms, and resources.

National Suicide Prevention Lifeline

Call 1-800-273-8255

suicidepreventionlifeline.org

Includes online chat options.

National Alliance on Mental Illness (NAMI)

nami.org

Provides advocacy, education, support, and public awareness so that all individuals and families affected by mental illness can build better lives.

EDUCATIONAL RESOURCES

International OCD Foundation

iocdf.org

Anxiety & Depression Association of America

adaa.org

WHAT IS THIS BOOK?

A few years ago, my boyfriend at the time was flying back to Los Angeles after some unmemorable trip. Airplanes have always been a big trigger for me, so I sat nervously in my apartment waiting for his estimated time of arrival. That time came and went. My anxiety kicked into high gear. I started calling and texting, desperate for proof that he had survived the flight. My fear was twofold: (1) He was definitely dead, along with two hundred other people, and (2) he was alive and well, but didn't care about me at all. I wasn't sure what was worse. Said boyfriend knew about my plane anxiety. He knew I worried he would die every time he boarded a plane. He knew I expected him to check in the moment he touched down. And yet . . . radio silence.

Not to completely ruin the suspense, but my boyfriend survived. (Our relationship did not.) When I finally got him on the phone, there was some long-forgotten explanation for the delay, most likely involving a dead phone battery. But by the time we connected, I was already inconsolable. Exhausted from traveling, he passively listened to me cry, unable or unwilling to understand my distress. He doesn't experience plane anxiety, so why should I? It's illogical! Planes are safer than cars! Of course he was going to get in touch *eventually*. Wasn't that obvious?!

Here's the thing: Logic and anxiety do not mix. They're like oil and water. Or pugs and strenuous exercise. Not a match! And if you aren't being forced to read this against your will, you already know that, because you've probably experienced something similar. It is one of the most basic tenets of mental illness. It's an *illness*! It doesn't make sense! For those of us with mental health issues, we not only have to live with this paradox, but we are also tasked with explaining it to our partners. This is pretty fucking annoying and more difficult than some might think. I think we can all agree that romantic relationships are challenging for everyone. But when you throw anxiety, OCD, and/or depression into the mix, the idea of "happily ever after" might feel more like a propaganda campaign than something actually achievable. I'm here to change your mind. Your dating history doesn't have to predict your dating future. While those of us with these conditions might have to work a bit harder at achieving healthy relationships, we are more than capable of doing so through self-awareness, expert communication, and productive dating (e.g., not wasting your time on the wrong people even if they're really, really, really good-looking).

Right about now you might be wondering, *This all sounds good, but who the hell are you?* My name's Allison, and I'm an author, screenwriter, podcaster, and (mostly former) YouTuber. I've also been battling my own brain since I was four years old. Until I got sick, I was a happy, carefree child. Easygoing. Down to party. And then I contracted strep throat. A few weeks later, my entire demeanor changed due to PANDAS—Pediatric Autoimmune Neuropsychiatric Disorders Associated with Streptococcal Infections. (Not the adorable bear, unfortunately.) Basically, the strep infection changed my brain, and I was suddenly so mentally unwell that I announced to my father, "I need to see a doctor. Something inside me is making me sad." Pretty astute for a preschooler, don't you think?! Also, very tragic and disturbing for my poor parents.

Within weeks, I was diagnosed with obsessive-compulsive disorder. According to the *Diagnostic and Statistical Manual of Mental Disorders, Fifth Edition* (DSM-5), obsessive-compulsive disorder is defined as a "presence of obsessions, compulsions, or both." Over the years, I've mostly battled with obsessions: "Recurrent and persistent thoughts, urges, or impulses that are experienced, at some time during the disturbance, as intrusive and unwanted, and that in most individuals cause marked anxiety or distress." As a kid, I was unable to touch the floor (contamination) or tell my parents I loved them (fear of lying). My otherwise completely privileged childhood was suddenly clouded by debilitating neurosis, self-hate, and depression that followed me into adulthood. Despite the fact that I was getting good grades, my parents almost had to pull me out of boarding school and, later, out of college, due to my deteriorating mental state. Again, not at all fun for my poor parents.

Despite my OCD and anxiety, I've been able to achieve significant career success as an adult. (Did you watch BuzzFeed videos circa 2015? I was one of the girls with bangs!) But no matter what progress I made in my career, there was one area of my life that remained a constant trigger and brought out the worst in me and my symptoms: romantic relationships. I have been guilty of every "crazy girl" stereotype out there. I've called too much. I've texted too much. I've stayed up all night crying, praying a boyfriend wasn't going to dump me in the morning. (He did.) I've tracked a different boyfriend's whereabouts through his Instagram activity.

I've repeatedly found myself too preoccupied with my life-partner obsession to take part in normal life and actually enjoy it. I've immediately jumped from one mediocre relationship to another to avoid a single extra second of being alone. I've even contemplated suicide more than once following a breakup. Since I was a kid, I've obsessively worried that I would be alone forever. And this near-debilitating fear permeated all aspects of my life and severely impacted my overall happiness and mental state.

But, I'm happy to report, things are different now. I no longer fall into the same harmful cycles and unhealthy relationship habits. I no longer associate my entire self-worth with my relationship status. And the most devastating breakup of my entire life (which happened while writing this very book) didn't destroy me. In fact, my resiliency following that heartbreak gave me even more confidence in what I'm about to share with you. Because I am living proof that we can change. That's the really good news. The less good (but still not bad) news is that change takes work. For me, that work included years of therapy, medication, behavioral control, cognitive restructuring, and elevating my self-esteem. It wasn't a shift that happened overnight, and it wasn't devoid of a lot of sweat and discomfort. In many ways, it's an ongoing battle. But I can assure you it's a battle worth fighting. And I hope you can take comfort in knowing your hard work will pay off, whether that means you successfully find a life partner or the thought of looking for one no longer makes you want to throw up from anxiety. Both are victories in my book! (Pun intended.)

There is already a lot of literature out there on how to find "the one." There are also numerous books about mental illness. But I don't think any have explicitly examined the link between the two. So that's what I'm doing here. This book provides clear-cut advice on how to form healthy dating and relationship habits when you live with OCD, anxiety, and/or depression. And, while a lot of the advice is helpful for people in every stage of relationships, we will be primarily focusing on new connections and the early stages of forming a partnership. Basically that nerve-wracking time frame between meeting someone and deciding whether or not to commit to a life partnership. I not only pull from my own experiences, but I also interview licensed therapists, relationship experts, and real-life couples for their points of view and professional guidance. I want you to be able to walk away from this book feeling less alone in the struggle *and* prepared to tackle dating and relationships with more confidence and less worry.

But I should warn you right now that despite a plethora of tangible tips and tricks, this book isn't a one-size-fits-all magical solution that guarantees you'll be married within the year. (If it were, I'd be a billionaire!) Everyone is different, and everyone's symptoms manifest differently. That's part of why I narrowed this book down to anxiety, OCD, and depression. These three disorders are just a sliver of the mental health spectrum, but they're all I can speak to personally. I also want to point out that my goal isn't for you to simply read this book, nod a few times, and go about your life. Just like in therapy, I want you to be an active participant along the way. While this isn't a workbook, there are personal exercises suggested throughout. It might be helpful to have a specific notebook nearby when reading this book so all your related thoughts are in one place. Plus, who doesn't love a new notebook!

I know this kind of self-examination can be daunting to think about. We often feel so stuck in our ways and our disorder(s) that there doesn't seem to be much of a point in even trying to change. But I'm happy to announce that we have much more control over our thoughts and behaviors than our neural pathways want us to believe. The first step in taking back control is building self-awareness. As much as people tell you to follow your heart when it comes to love, the reality is that your partner is going to be in a relationship with your brain. That's why it's important to figure out how your individual brain works. How can you expect someone to understand you and anticipate your reactions if you can't do the same for yourself? (Trick question! You can't!)

When sitting down to write this book, I was forced to examine something I had never really thought about before: *Why* did I crave a life partner so badly? Why did this one desire rule my life above all else? The only explanation that made any sense was a deep fear that without said partner, I would never be truly happy. I was not enough alone. I was broken and have been broken since my first diagnosis at age four. And, according to societal lore, true love has magical qualities. So when nothing else (medication, therapy, positive self-talk) worked, I could hold on to the hope that love would fix me. If someone special picked *me* to share their life with, I would suddenly hold value. I would be "normal." I would finally find peace inside my own brain.

Obviously, none of that is true. All humans inherently hold value and no one's worth is tied to another's approval. "Normal" is just a social construct. And romantic love may be a wonderful, beautiful thing, but it is not the sole indicator of a life well lived. The longest relationship you will ever have is the one you have with yourself. You want to make sure it is one full of love, respect, and compassion. It took me a long time to figure that out. But once I got there, it was like a weight had been lifted and I was able to move about the world more freely, with or without a partner. (Even though I would prefer to have a partner.)

Rest assured that this book will not have a twist ending. It won't lead you down a path that promises romantic success only to proclaim, "You don't need romantic love! You just need to love yourself!" In fact, part of what I want to accomplish with this book is to break the stigma that there is something inherently wrong with wanting and actively seeking a life partner. Desiring romantic love does not mean you are not good enough on your own. When you break it down, it's really just a lifestyle choice, and we shouldn't judge one another on our preferred lifestyles. Instead of feeling ashamed, you should feel empowered that you care about yourself enough to go after what you want. It's an act of bravery to allow yourself the joy that comes with romantic love. The reality is that it takes a lot of risk to love and be loved. And just because we have been deprived of joy at times throughout our lives due to our mental health doesn't mean we should stop fighting for happiness. If anything, it should motivate us to fight harder. The world is metaphorically—and in some places, quite literally—burning around us. We need to reach for all the happiness we can. So from this sentence forward, let's all agree to love love and feel stronger, not weaker, for it!

Despite your worst thoughts and fears, people who struggle with their mental health are more than capable of successfully dating and maintaining long-term relationships. It simply requires a bit more of that sweat and discomfort I mentioned earlier. But I believe those who have had to work hard on themselves make the best partners, because they know happiness doesn't come easily. They understand that when you catch it, it's something to celebrate and nurture. I know that if you're reading this book, your journey to find love has been hard and sometimes unbearable. But please keep reading! There is hope at the end of this dark and confusing tunnel. It's going to be a wild ride, but we'll be in it together.

CHAPTER ONE

HOW CAN I HANDLE BREAKUPS BETTER?

MEET THE EXPERTS:

- **Dr. Robin Gibbs** is a clinical psychologist specializing in the treatment of trauma. She is trained in many state-of-the-art treatments, including eye movement desensitization and reprocessing (EMDR), sensorimotor psychotherapy, acceptance and commitment therapy (ACT), and internal family systems (IFS), but prioritizes her relationships with her clients. She uses mindfulness and coherent breathing to help clients manage anxiety and regulate moods. She also enjoys writing and speaking to a wide range of audiences. We'll be referring to her as Robin.

- **Dr. Joanna Robin, PhD**, is a licensed clinical psychologist and the founder and director of the Westchester Anxiety Treatment Psychological Services in White Plains, New York. An expert in cognitive behavioral therapy (CBT), she specializes in the treatment of anxiety, mood, and behavioral problems in children, adolescents, and adults. She is the coauthor of *The OCD Workbook for Kids: Skills to Help Children Manage Obsessive Thoughts and Compulsive Behaviors* and has coauthored numerous publications on CBT, anxiety, parenting, and emotion regulation. She also provides a range of workshops and trainings on anxiety, OCD, CBT for anxiety and disruptive behavior disorders, parenting, and stress management. We'll be referring to her as Joanna.

The first time I cut my skin with a razor blade, I was a sophomore in college. I'd used physical pain as a coping mechanism since I was a little kid, but until that point it was confined to pinching, hitting, and scratching. Those methods no longer seemed like enough to successfully shift my focus away from my emotions. So I took my overpriced pink razor for ladies and sliced my hips until they bled. What caused this upgrade in self-harm? My college boyfriend of seven months no longer wanted to be with me. And that was enough to make me wish I was dead. So I escalated my self-harm to numb the pain.

When I asked Dr. Robin Gibbs, clinical psychologist and trauma specialist, why breakups are so exceptionally triggering for our mental health, she laughed and replied, "You mean aside from rejection? A universal source of agony for the entire human race? You mean aside from that?" She makes a good point! I think we can all agree rejection sucks. The simple fear of rejection is so overwhelming that it can stop people from going after what they want. But unless you completely withdraw from the world and live in a cave, rejection is inevitable. Especially when you open yourself up to love.

The lowest moments of my life have always followed romantic rejection. Nothing could rip apart my mental health faster, not even dirty hotel rooms (although those are a close second). Every time I put myself "back out there," it felt dangerous. Reckless. Could I mentally survive another heartbreak? Would I even be able to find another person I liked enough that they could break my heart?! Fortunately, humans are far more resilient than we are led to believe. But that doesn't mean we shouldn't do everything we can to protect ourselves. This protection includes reframing how we approach the entire idea of breakups and learning better coping mechanisms. For a long time, I thought if someone I liked or loved didn't like or love me back, that meant, without a doubt, that I was an unlovable piece of shit. I was worthless and disgusting. No one else would want to touch me with a ten-foot pole. When I expressed this reaction to Robin, she understood where I was coming from: "Who wants to feel that somebody knows them and is like, 'Yeah, no thank you'? It's a devastatingly painful experience. And if you already are not feeling so confident and comfortable with yourself, it's even more painful." So basically it makes sense that a breakup has the ability to negatively rock your world, especially if you're on unstable ground to begin with.

But what can we do to prevent ourselves from going to the darkest corners of our brains? How do we defend ourselves against the somewhat inevitable without giving up on the pursuit of love? Sometimes the first step is understanding why you are hurting so badly. I know I always felt pathetic for being so distraught. What kind of independent woman lets a straight, cis man affect her this much? I am a disappointment to the feminist movement! There must be something wrong with me on some fundamental level, right? According to Dr. Joanna Robin, who specializes in anxiety and cognitive behavioral therapy (CBT), it's a lot more complicated than that. When you lose a partner, Joanna says, "It's not just your boyfriend or girlfriend, it's your best friend. You're losing your best friend who you talk to every day, see every day, sleep with every night. It's quite traumatic. It's not like any other relationship that ends." Turns out, I wasn't just some boy-obsessed loser. I was responding to true loss. And unless you've managed to completely disconnect from your emotions, that loss is going to hurt. A lot. So any self-judgment that follows your reaction to heartbreak is unnecessary and misinformed. You are hurting and that is normal. Cut yourself some slack and a big piece of cake.

Here's a question: Have any of you ever felt this type of hurt following the end of something that was nowhere near a real relationship and thought, *What the fuck?!* Maybe it's rejection after a few dates. Maybe it's rejection before you even get the chance to date. And somehow it still hurts as if you'd been married to that near stranger for decades? Once, in my early twenties, I finally got together with a guy I'd liked for years. It was one of those incredible days where an afternoon coffee led into eight straight hours of hanging out and making out. I was smitten! I was in love! (No, I wasn't.) I was sure it was the real deal! Three days later, while I was in Chicago to shoot a Payless ShoeSource commercial, I noticed he was barely responding to my witty texts. After some badgering, he confessed it just wasn't going to work out. We were over before we even started. I was devastated. And embarrassed. How could I be so distraught after *three days*? Luckily, my therapist gave me some much-needed perspective. She said I was so upset because I was losing *the fantasy* of him. And that fantasy was something I'd been toying with for years. It was meaningful to me. So the next time someone abruptly ends things and it stings more than you'd expect, try to remember that losing the possibility of something can be just as painful as losing the actual thing. And then eat another piece of cake!

Moving on to more long-term relationships: I think there are three different ways people break up. Your partner initiates it. You initiate it. Or you mutually agree to consciously uncouple. (I'm going to mostly ignore that third option.) Each type comes with its own unique complications. Let's start off dissecting the first option. You've gotten dumped. And it fucking sucks. I've been dumped many, many (many) times. And my immediate response is always, *How do I make them realize they've made a huge mistake? How do I get them back? How do I avoid this pain that is so awful and uncomfortable?* Coinciding with this line of unhelpful thinking is a deep, dark spiral that often starts with, *So-and-so doesn't want to marry me; therefore, I will never get married, I will never experience love again, I will be unhappy for the rest of my life, my face is disgusting* . . . You know! A deep, dark spiral that gets wider and deeper as more and more unhelpful and untrue thoughts pile on.

I asked Robin how to combat this dangerous rabbit hole before you fall all the way down. She said, "The first step always is noticing the thoughts that then lead to the feelings of despair, sadness, hopelessness, and shame. And try to notice it as a thought rather than a fact. The sequence is always noticing, labeling, grounding back to this moment." Anxiety, depression, and OCD love to mislabel thoughts as facts. It's their most powerful trick. So it's your job throughout the day, maybe even dozens of times a day, to listen to what your mind is telling you and decide if it's actually a fact or just a thought. Because facts are information we can learn from to adjust or inform our behavior in the future. Thoughts, on the other hand, hold the same weight as dreams. They're in our brain, so they seem real, but they're not. They're quite literally figments of our imagination.

Let's play a quick game of Fact or Thought, shall we?

Mind: My partner dumped me because they don't think we have long-term potential.
Correct label: Fact.

Mind: If my partner can't see long-term potential with me, no one will.
Correct label: Thought.

Mind: I loved my ex more than I have loved anyone else I've ever dated.
Correct label: Fact. (Assuming you're self-aware enough to know this.)

Mind: I will never love anyone else as much as I love my ex.
Correct label: Thought. (How do you know?! You haven't even tried!)

After years of therapy and medication, I can assure you that you will never fully be able to prevent yourself from thinking an unhelpful, incorrect thought. But you *can* learn how to ignore it immediately afterward, which is almost the same thing.

Another harmful game we tend to play with ourselves after being dumped is called "What if?" What if I hadn't said that thing that led to that argument? What if we had met when we were younger instead? What if we had met when we were older instead? What if I liked staying up until 2:00 a.m. and doing cocaine instead of going to bed early and not doing cocaine? (That last one might be specific just to me.) We've all played various versions of this game. Robin points out that sometimes it's a useful way to prepare ourselves: "'What if there's an earthquake in California? I guess I should have a plan in place.' That's productive. Great! As long as you don't live in that. You get your plan, you have your go bag, and you're done with it. But when it becomes a loop over and over again, it really makes us sick. It causes all kinds of stress hormones to be released. The challenge is to notice it, acknowledge it, and ground yourself back in the present moment."

It's honestly commendable that our brain is working overtime to solve the problem of losing someone we love. Unfortunately, it's just wasted energy, because all of the solutions the what-if thoughts come up with are impossible to implement. You can't take back an argument. You can't magically change your life's timeline. As Joanna puts it, "Your brain is trying to help you problem-solve a problem that can't be solved. It makes it more likely you're going to ruminate." So not only do these types of what-if thoughts not accomplish anything positive, they also increase the likelihood that you're going to waste hours of your life and far too many stress hormones replaying useless scenarios. What happened, happened. It's best to accept that and, whenever possible, learn from the experience. According to Robin, "The goal is to take what serves you and leave behind the rest." After every breakup, take the time to examine what you've learned about yourself, what you've learned about the type of relationship that works for you, and what you've learned in terms of how you want to act in the future. Write it down. Ingest it. Then, as Elsa and every child born after 2010 likes to belt, you have to let it go(ooooo).

. . . But what if you can't let it go? What if everyone tells you "time heals all wounds" but it's been three years and you're still obsessed with your ex? Maybe you're even dating someone new but you still insist on grilling a mutual friend for information every chance you get? Maybe you check your ex's social media constantly, or ruminate in the shower day after day after day about a scenario where your ex shows up and asks for you back? Maybe you contact said ex the moment you break up with that someone new, even though your ex is dating someone else and has major commitment issues? Maybe you tell yourself that these years apart will just make your story even more powerful once your ex finally realizes you're the only one for them? In case it's not blatantly obvious, I was obsessed with an ex for years and most definitely did all of those things. Shout-out to my mid to late twenties! Don't miss ya!

Eighty percent of the time I found it extremely distressing that I could not get over this specific person. Twenty percent of the time I was convinced it must "mean something." My brain was trying to explain away my obsession by turning our failed relationship into the greatest love story of all time—or at least the greatest love story of my time/life. In reality, I wasn't unable to move on because he was so special. I was unable to move on because I kept avoiding the work involved in getting over someone. As Joanna puts it, "I think time heals all wounds if you're doing things that will make you healthier. So if you're checking their social media a lot, if you're staying in touch in some ways, you're not letting yourself heal. I don't think time is going to be enough." Basically, you can't move forward if one foot is still stuck in their bullshit. You have to break free completely before time can take over and work its magic.

Robin goes a bit further in explaining why it might be hard to move on even after a considerable amount of time: "One theory I would have is that it's hooking into an older trauma, which is keeping it alive. As a trauma therapist, my recommendation would be that you have to heal the older stuff that keeps the current stuff going. People who don't have a lot of trauma in their past have a much easier time hurting and then moving forward." On the one hand, this is discouraging to hear because it means some of us might have to do some more in-depth work to heal. On the other hand, it's further proof that this specific person isn't the issue, and we should assign less power to them. If you have an open wound, someone only needs to flick you for the pain to be excruciating. It doesn't mean they are stronger than anyone else or they are your one true love. I know this conflicts with a lot of movies and books that glorify pain, but try to trust me. Love doesn't have to be hard, despite what your societally influenced brain tells you.

OCD in particular likes to convince us of false narratives that conflict with reality and cause unnecessary heartache. Let's say, for example, that you've started dating someone new and you occasionally miss your ex. This is a very normal, human feeling. You spent a lot of time with that person. You're going to occasionally miss them. But your OCD might spin those harmless feelings into something much more nefarious. OCD has a tendency to hate anything that isn't extremely clear-cut. So in order to avoid the discomfort that often comes with complex emotions, your OCD might add extra meaning to certain feelings: If you miss your ex *at all*, your OCD might extrapolate that to mean you don't like your current partner enough, when the two aren't related. Joanna adds that OCD "makes up rules in those types of situations, and you're like, 'Oh that makes total sense, OCD, of course, that's a rule.' But OCD makes up pretend rules." Say it again for the people in the back: OCD MAKES UP PRETEND RULES!!!

We need to do our best to remember that X does not inherently equal Y, even if our brain is continuously shouting, "X equals Y!

Look, I solved it! X equals Y!" Just because your new relationship might feel different than the one before it doesn't mean it lacks the potential to flourish into something even better. As humans, we love to ascribe meaning to everything, but sometimes that does us a huge disservice. A lot of times a new relationship might feel less exciting simply because it's healthy! There isn't the agonizing push and pull you had with that jerk who didn't want to commit but liked to Netflix and chill occasionally. You're not experiencing a roller coaster of emotions every twelve hours for days on end. You're not so confused about their intentions that you're rereading every text conversation fifty times. So your OCD or anxiety tries to make sense of this big change and falsely decides, "You don't like this new person enough." When in reality, drama does not equal love. Oftentimes, it means the exact opposite.

While it's normal to compare new partners to past partners, try to remember no two people are the same; therefore, no two relationships will feel the same. Plus, you are changing all the time! The way you feel after a first kiss when you're fifteen is going to be vastly different than how you feel when you're twenty-nine or forty-two. (For example, I didn't know I had to breathe through my nose during my first kiss at fifteen, so afterward I felt yucky and light-headed. Pretty cool!) I know that according to my social security number, I am technically the same person I was when I was nineteen and my college boyfriend dumped me, but I've also learned so many things and had so many new experiences since then that it's often hard to relate to that person. We don't have the same worldview anymore. We don't have the same emotional life. That's why I don't romanticize people from my past—chances are we aren't even compatible anymore, if we ever were! Try to let the fact that you've grown be the closure you need from your past relationships.

Before we move on to scenario two (you initiate the breakup), I want to acknowledge how discouraging it can feel when you've made significant progress on your mental health, only for a breakup to throw you off course. You might feel like, *Ugh! I put in all this time and energy to better myself and now I'm back to square one! What's the freakin' point?* Robin says one thing that can help combat this feeling of hopelessness is maintaining a wider perspective: "Life is like the weather. Sometimes there are going to be terrible storms. And when there's a storm outside, it's not about making that go away. We don't have any control over that. It's about weathering the storm. And when you truly are heartbroken or are suffering from a loss, it really hurts. That is just life. We want to live fully, but that also means feeling the bad stuff. A routine is really good for your mental health. Pushing yourself through exercise really does help. Eating even when you don't really want to eat. Because that is what your body needs to weather the storm."

Even when you've hit rock bottom, try to remember what techniques and coping mechanisms have benefited you in the past. Does going for a long walk while listening to a podcast help ease your anxiety? What about talking to someone in your support system? Maybe you want to get back into exercising regularly? Another option to consider is medication if it's helped you before or if you think it might improve your functioning. We'll dive into medication more later (see chapter five), but keep in mind, it can be a short-term treatment and not something you have to take for the rest of your life. When we're in crisis, we need to do whatever needs to be done to stay alive. I know that sounds dramatic, but for a lot of us with mental health struggles, that's simply our reality. We have to figure out how to claw our way back to wanting to live. And part of that is *actively deciding* that we are worth nurturing through self-care. So be kind to yourself, try to go to sleep at a reasonable hour, and remember to drink lots of water. We have to care for our bodies in order to heal our minds.

I've always found it helpful to equate emotional problems to physical problems. It makes it harder to judge yourself. After all, no one ever shouts at someone to just "get over" a broken leg. (At least I hope they don't.) After a major heartbreak, you're not yourself. You need to build up your stamina again. You need to train your brain. As Joanna puts it, "If you have an injury, you have to do rehab or physical therapy. It's not just going to get better. For a broken heart, you have to actually take care of yourself physically, emotionally. I always equate it to running or doing a plank or something. You feel like you can't do it, you can't get there, and the more you say, 'I can't do it, I can't get there,' you're going to walk, you're not going to run. You're not gonna hold the plank. But the more you remind yourself of your strength and your resilience, the more you are going to be able to get through it. It's not that it's not hard. It's very hard." So try not to make things harder by engaging in negative self-talk. Lift yourself up instead of pulling yourself down. Recognize your starting point and visualize your goal. And before you know it, you'll be doing pull-ups! (Just kidding! Those are way too hard, but maybe you'll be able to go to a party without crying!)

———

We've officially covered what to do and what not to do when you get dumped. But for a lot of people, doing the dumping is just as awful and debilitating. Unless you're a sadist, it feels pretty terrible to hurt someone. Especially when you care (or cared) deeply about them. Plus, no one wants to feel like the villain. It's a yucky, icky feeling most people try to avoid at all costs. But I'm here to tell you, breaking up with someone doesn't automatically make you a bad person. It simply makes you a person who recognizes the need for a positive change. Now, breaking up with someone over text and then banging their best friend right after? That's a bit harder to defend.

For those of us with anxiety or a beating heart, it can be agonizing trying to decide whether or not to end a relationship, which means the breaking-up process often starts long before you arrive at your final decision. It's one thing if you're fighting all the time and it's clearly toxic, but what if you're relatively happy in the day-to-day yet you don't see a long-term future? What if your partner is awesome but for whatever reason you're just not that into it anymore? Chances are, if you're reading this book, you're going to ruminate and ruminate and ruminate. Not only are you debating the value of the relationship, but you might also be wondering if you're mentally strong enough to go through another breakup. I'll be the first to admit that I've been relatively unhappy with someone but stayed because I needed to build up the mental strength to handle a huge change. Has anyone else done this? Anyone?? ANYONE?! Luckily for me, Robin says this scenario is "not uncommon at all." And somewhat surprisingly, her advice isn't to simply buck up and end things right away. Depending on the situation and assuming the relationship isn't toxic, Robin says, "The goal might be to try to figure out what you need in order to be able to let go." So that might mean therapy. That might mean finding a new job. That might just mean you need a bit more time to get used to the idea. Check in with yourself and figure out what you need to do to comfortably take that next step without the fear that you'll never recover.

Another big reason people put off breaking up is the worry that their partner will hurt themselves as a result. This might be an unsubstantiated fear or the result of someone explicitly stating, "If you leave, I will kill myself." Either way, it's a terrible position to be in and it's extraordinarily unhealthy—for both of you. Robin explains, "It's never good to feel coerced in that way. The fact is, we're not responsible for keeping the other person alive. That's destructive for both of you. It doesn't help your partner for you to just be in a relationship for that reason." It's strange to hear a mental health professional tell you that you're not morally responsible for keeping another person alive. Isn't that the right thing to do? Shouldn't we always do everything in our power to save someone else? Yes and no.

If you're worried your partner might hurt themselves if you leave, you should do your best to make sure they have a support system ready to step in following the breakup. This can be their friends, family, and/or a therapist. I once broke up with a boyfriend in his therapist's office. Things had been bad for a while and I was worried about his safety. It was honestly a huge relief to be able to say to a professional, "I can't handle this anymore. Can you please help instead?" I walked away sobbing, but with relief that someone was looking out for him. I also called a mutual friend on the ride home so she could check in on him as well. I was lucky that there were other people around who cared about him so I could easily pass the baton.

But what do you do if *you* are your partner's entire support system? Maybe they have a shitty family or don't have any true friends. They make you feel like you are the only person they have in the entire world and now you're going to leave them too??? What are you, a monster?! Nope. Robin says that even in this scenario, "The goal is to get out of the relationship." You just want to make sure you do so with compassion: "Make it lovingly clear that what's

.

going on is not helpful to either of you. For the person who is not struggling, that kind of emotional coercion is too much of a burden and responsibility to carry. Sometimes if it really heats up, it's about calling the crisis team in your local community." So take yourself off the hook, find your partner other avenues of support, and remember it's the right decision for both of you. Your soon-to-be ex-partner deserves someone who wants to be there just as much as you deserve someone you want to be with.

Let's move on to a less high-stakes scenario. You're not afraid your partner is going to harm themselves, but you're still struggling with guilt and anxiety over ending the relationship. You feel like you're a bad person. That you're being selfish. Joanna argues that ending a relationship isn't inherently selfish: "I talk a lot about selfish versus self-preserving. Are you being selfish, or are you taking care of yourself? We can't be in a relationship that is not working. Guilt is a good emotion for when we've hurt someone and we could have prevented it. But sometimes we need to be self-preserving and take care of ourselves, even if this may mean that we disappoint others." As someone who used to be fueled entirely by guilt, anxiety, and cleaning compulsions, it took me a long time to understand that putting myself first didn't inherently make me selfish. Instead, it allowed me to grow into the best version of myself. And that person is better able to care for others because she's not constantly falling apart.

If it's not that easy for you to shed the feeling of being selfish, Robin suggests examining the source of your guilt: "What is it signaling? What is it trying to say to you? Were you somehow given the message that other people's feelings are more important than yours? Did you have experiences early on in your life where you were given the message that it's your job to take care of people emotionally? If so, you want to really explore that. Is that serving you today?" She goes on to further explain how important it is to unlearn incorrect assumptions we made as children: "If you happen to have a parent with mental illness or alcoholism and you got the message that it's your job to be the caretaker, it gets frozen in time from the point when it develops. So, for an eight-year-old, that makes perfect sense: 'Oh yeah, it's my job to make sure Mommy's happy or Mommy's not depressed.' The problem is that it stays with you, so you then develop this strategy that to be loved, you need to be the caretaker. In which case it would not be a good thing to leave somebody who needs you. But we adults know better. The adult perspective is that it's really important to take care of your own mental health."

She brings up two huge questions I think we all need to write down in our notebooks:

1 Do I have an adult perspective on how healthy relationships work?

2 Do I think other people's feelings are more important than mine?

The short answers we are looking for are yes and no. And if those aren't your answers, you've discovered something about yourself that is in need of further exploration. This is actually a good thing. You now have some more insight into what's potentially fueling your unhealthy thoughts, feelings, or behaviors. Self-awareness is an important step, even if we don't always love what we find. (Turns out, I used to hate other women because I was jealous of them. That was a lot of fun to unpack!)

In our continuing hypothetical situation, you have officially decided that you are going to break up with your partner. Now how the hell do you do it? And don't you dare say "text" or I'll send you into a five-minute time-out and take your phone away. Even if the thought of it makes you anxious, my advice—out of courtesy to your partner—is to do it in person with a preplanned idea of what you're going to say. Know and be able to articulate your reasons for ending the relationship. While the truth can hurt, I find it to be less harmful in the long term than leaving someone with nothing but confusion. We all know how much anxiety likes to feed off uncertainty, so don't let there be any. Give your partner the gift of clarity. And, perhaps most importantly, make sure you give them time to share how they're feeling. You're already disrupting their sense of stability by making a unilateral decision, so it's important to let them say their piece. This way, they (hopefully) won't feel bulldozed. Stay respectful. Stay compassionate. And don't engage if they try to lure you into a fight. Remain calm and remember that everything they're saying is coming from a place of hurt. Also, make sure you have an escape plan. For example, don't do this on vacation or in the middle of traffic. The metaphorical exit sign should be clearly marked for both of you.

———

Congratulations! Your unsatisfying relationship is officially over! Or is it? There is a lot of debate on whether or not exes should stay in touch. My personal belief is no. Cut ties! Mute their socials! Pretend they never existed! Just joshing about the last one. But I do think there should be a period of time where you don't talk. If you want to get back in touch a few months later? Go for it. But when the wound is fresh, I find it's best to heal in private. If you keep in touch the whole time, you're still going to be taking their thoughts and feelings into account on a daily basis. This can prevent you from discovering what it means to live your life without them. Plus, having some time away might help give you a better perspective on what you've learned from that relationship—both the good and the bad.

That said, everyone is different, so this is another case of "figure out what's right for you"! Start by asking yourself how you currently feel about your partner. Do you still have feelings for them? Or did the love/lust die long before the death of your relationship? Joanna says if the romantic/physical attraction is gone and it's turned into more of a loving, sibling-like relationship, it can be healthy to stay in touch. But if one person is still holding a torch, keeping in touch isn't a great idea. In fact, it's only going to extend the healing process. If you're the one holding the torch, you're allowed to say you want some time without talking, even if your partner "really wants to stay friends!" This is you setting up a boundary, and according to Robin, "Everyone is born entitled to have a boundary." I think this is something we all know conceptually but have a hard time sticking to in practice. If maintaining boundaries is something you struggle with, might I recommend tattooing "everyone is born entitled to have a boundary" on your arm? If needles scare you, you can just turn it into a daily mantra instead. It's got a nice flow to it.

Now, what's the protocol if you are over the romantic part of the relationship but your ex isn't? I personally think it becomes your responsibility to cut off communication. When I've said this to friends in the past, I've been met with resistance that sounded a lot like, "If they don't want to talk to me anymore, they can tell me. Why do I have to cut off contact if I'm fine with it?" Short answer?

Because it's the right thing to do. It's obviously not your legal obligation to cut someone loose, but a lot of people don't have enough willpower to disconnect even when they know keeping in touch is detrimental to their healing. If you recognize that that's what's going on with your ex, do them a favor and set up a—drumroll please—BOUNDARY!!

The final tricky part of breaking up, whether you are the dumper or the dumpee, is knowing when and how much to lean on friends and family for support. As someone who has historically spiraled into depression following heartbreak, I often feel like I can be a lot to handle. I want their help when I'm in crisis, but I also don't want to overload them with my problems. Following a breakup, Robin says, "It's important to reach out to your friends and family. Of course you need to lean on them just like they lean on you when they're in pain and struggling. But don't forget that putting one foot in front of the other really belongs to you. Other people are your secondary helpers." Call your friends, cry to your family, and methodically pet your dog. But don't expect anyone else to fix you or make the pain instantly go away. That's on you, unfortunately. Even though I know your dog would help if they could.

It's also important to be cognizant of your friends' reactions when you come to them for help. Joanna says that if your friends keep giving you the same advice over and over again, "It sounds like maybe your friends have exhausted what they have to offer and they might feel frustrated that they tried to give you advice and it hasn't worked. Sometimes we just want to vent and we want them to listen, but sometimes it makes them feel helpless. They can't help you, so they try to give advice. And if they're giving advice and you're not listening, it can feel frustrating for them because they don't feel helpful and our friends want to help us." We've all had that friend who asks us a million times for our advice and then doesn't listen to that advice, and I think we can agree it's infuriating after a while. So let's do our best to not be that friend. (Anymore.) Plus, when you constantly bring up the same points to a friend over and over, you're subconsciously asking them to participate in your rumination. You are basically using another person to help fuel your spiral. And that's not fair to them or healthy for you. So instead of making your friend rehash for the fiftieth time every stupid thing your ex ever said, invite them over for a movie night. Nurture yourself with the mere presence of their company. And maybe after a Bridget Jones double feature, you'll feel a little bit bet-' ter. (Sub in whatever double feature brings you joy! *Terminator 1* and *2? Terminator 2* and *3? Terminator 3* and *4?* Wow, there have been a lot of Terminators!)

And thus concludes our breakup chapter. Let's do a quick highlights tour of what we've learned. (And if you're thinking, *I'LL NEVER HAVE ANOTHER RELATIONSHIP EVER AGAIN THERE IS NO POINT IN ME READING THE REST OF THIS BOOK*, feel free to review this whole chapter one more time! We've all been in that mental spiral, and sometimes it takes longer than we'd like to snap out of it. There is no shame in that!) Okay! Here. We. Go:

- It's normal to be completely devastated following a breakup. It's a loss unlike any other kind of relationship. Plus, rejection blows! That's just science.

- It can be just as painful to lose the *fantasy* of someone as it is to lose that actual someone.

- Learn to distinguish between facts and thoughts.

- Don't engage in what-ifs unless it's to prepare for some sort of natural disaster. And even then, just prepare your go bag and move on.

- OCD loves to make up rules! That doesn't mean you should listen to them.

- You should never stay in a relationship solely because you're afraid of hurting the other person or of the other person hurting themselves.

- Learn to distinguish between selfishness and self-preservation.

- It takes real work to heal from heartbreak. Eat. Sleep. Exercise. Repeat.

- If you want to break up with someone, do it clearly and in person. Give them time to express their thoughts and feelings.

- Explore any residual feelings before deciding to stay in touch with an ex.

- You're entitled to boundaries! Use them!

- Lean on your friends, but don't trample them. Remember you have to do the real work yourself.

- Keep a wide perspective. A breakup isn't going to break you. It's just another storm you have to weather, and you've weathered storms before.

- Never break up with someone while stuck in traffic. Trust me.

See you on the next page! Great work, everyone!

WHAT'S ME AND WHAT'S MY DISORDER?

ne of the hardest parts of living with anxiety, OCD, and/or depression is figuring out who you really are underneath the bullshit (illness). So often the symptoms of these disorders look and *feel* like personality traits. For a long time, I thought I was "uptight." It turns out, I just didn't have a good handle on my anxiety. Many people with clinical depression might feel "antisocial," but they're actually experiencing the symptoms of a depressive episode. You can often lose sight of yourself if you've lived with

some form of mental illness for long enough. Why does that matter so much in a book about romantic relationships? Dating is hard enough on a good day, but imagine trying to date when you don't fully know who you are and, more importantly, which of your thoughts to trust. While it might sound like we only have one voice in our head, those of us with anxiety, OCD, and/or depression have two. One is our true self and the other is our illness yakking away at all hours while we're just trying to get some rest and watch reality TV. In this chapter, I'm going to try to help you learn to distinguish between those different voices so you can go forth and prosper (participate in healthy and happy romantic relationships).

My friend Liza has struggled with OCD since childhood, first showing symptoms as a toddler and finally getting diagnosed at age eight. She's now in her thirties and living with her partner, Brett, in Los Angeles. Despite having been with Brett for years, Liza still battles with the question, *Is he the right one for me?* While this might seem like a logical thing to occasionally ask yourself when in a relationship, Liza asks herself this question over and over and— you get the point.

In addition to general obsessive-compulsive disorder, Liza has a thematic subset of OCD called relationship OCD, or ROCD. According to Sheva Rajaee, a licensed marriage and family therapist who specializes in OCD and anxiety disorders, "OCD is a neurobiological condition with the presence of obsessions and compulsions. You have to have obsessions and compulsions to have OCD. The same goes for ROCD. ROCD is a theme that specifically fixates on whether or not you have all the right feelings for your partner, or if they have all the right feelings for you."

ROCD can manifest in two ways. This first is relationship-focused: *Am I good enough? Do they love me? Is my relationship satisfying enough?* The second is partner-focused: *Are* they *good enough? Do I love* them? Sheva mostly encounters partner-focused ROCD, which is what Liza continues to struggle with.

ROCD is different from normal doubts. It's incessant and often has harmful effects on romantic relationships. I drove down to Irvine, California, to get a better understanding of this thematic subset from Sheva in person. In addition to being an OCD therapist, Sheva also has OCD and ROCD herself, which she openly discusses with her patients. (This shocked me since I know absolutely nothing about my own therapist, other than she maybe once had a dog.) Sheva is young, stylish, and recently married. I'd say I want to be like her when I grow up, but we might be the same age.

My goal in talking to Sheva was to try to get to the heart of ROCD. Apparently, ROCD is most often triggered in viable relationships. Basically, your brain isn't going to bother to worry obsessively if someone is the right person for you when they only text you once every three months. ROCD is more likely to rear its ugly head when you're with someone you might actually have a future with. Sheva explains that this reaction comes from the threat or fear of getting hurt. You can get hurt through rejection. You can get hurt through being vulnerable. You can be vulnerable, which can lead to you getting rejected, which causes you to get hurt. Sheva says, "The actual core fear can be different for everyone, but it's usually a fear of vulnerability that is underscored by something else—fear of getting hurt, fear of making the wrong decision, fear of future regret." So instead of letting someone get close to you, you take one step forward and two steps back. You constantly worry you're making a huge mistake. You stare at their nose for hours on end and wonder, *Can I really look at this nose for fifty more years?* And then the next day, their nose looks adorable and you're fucking exhausted from the mental back and forth. DOES THIS SOUND FAMILIAR?

Unfortunately, one of the casualties of ROCD can be your relationship. According to Sheva, ROCD can look a lot like fear of commitment: "When you doubt something so completely [that] you disconnect from yourself, you're also going to disconnect from the relationship. So there is this sad distancing that happens. Sometimes it feels like you're hot and cold. Maybe one day your anxiety is in check for whatever reason—maybe you slept well and you're feeling really good and you're able to connect more completely with your partner. But a lot of times when you're anxious and your partner's the trigger, you're going to back off." This can be confusing and hurtful to your partner, causing a "natural wearing down of the partnership under the weight of these doubts."

ROCD can also get in the way of intimacy and sex. People with ROCD are often too caught up in intrusive thoughts to enjoy their sex life. It's hard to focus on your partner when all you can think is, *Does this feel right? Are we kissing enough? Would I rather be having sex with someone else?* I can tell you from personal experience that this kind of thinking is a total buzzkill in the bedroom.

So what the hell do you do? If you think or know you have ROCD, it's important to recognize those thoughts when they're coming up. But how can you determine your ROCD thoughts from valid concerns about the relationship? You don't want to end up sweeping real issues under the rug because you happen to have obsessive-compulsive disorder. When I interviewed Liza at my kitchen table, she said that despite learning about ROCD years ago, she still struggles with correctly categorizing her worries. "At this point, if I think about it too much, I will have an episode, and by episode, I mean anxiety. Anxiety to the point of physical discomfort," Liza confesses. It's true. I could see her tensing up the more we talked about it. Once you realize you have ROCD, it can seem impossible to determine the difference between understandable concerns and ROCD.

While Sheva admits this is always going to be murky territory, she offers some ways to help distinguish between the two. First, you want to look out for toxicity, which is emotional or physical abuse. If this is happening in your relationship, it's cause for real concern and not something you should ever chalk up to overthinking. You're responding to a real threat that you need to address. If your relationship isn't toxic, you want to examine the *way* the worry presents itself. Sheva says if it's "really repetitive, tens to hundreds of times a day—that incessancy can be uniquely OCD." On top of that, "ROCD fixates on issues that a more neurotypical person might overlook or not consider a big deal. Like the sound of their partner's voice or whether or not they'll still be in love with their partner in thirty years." She says you can look at the *content* of the worry to help you determine the cause. Is your worry something that's actually fixable, or is it more irrational?

Let's try to list some things that are most likely ROCD worries:

- Why is their laugh so loud?

- Why don't I like how they smell?

- Would I be better off with my ex?

- Would I be better off with my barista?

Now let's try to list some things that are most likely valid concerns:

- They don't listen to me.

- We never go on dates anymore.

- I feel like they prioritize their friends over me.

- I don't like the way they talk about my family.

As you can see, ROCD worries aren't things you can fix with the help of your partner. You can't sit down and say, "I think your laugh is too loud so my friends will hate you" and solve anything. All you'll do is unnecessarily hurt your partner's feelings. The valid concerns, on the other hand, are issues you can and should bring up and work together to solve. However, if your partner does the work to solve a concern along with three other worries you've brought up and you're *still* not satisfied, it might actually be that pesky ROCD.

If you suspect you have ROCD, I suggest creating a list of your concerns about your current partner and deciding what category they each fall into. (Not to get too fancy, but gel pens are very fun when making a list. Might I suggest hot pink for ROCD worries and a bold blue for valid concerns?) Defining your worries can help you determine what you should actually bring up to your partner and (hopefully) gives less power to your ROCD thoughts by recognizing them as such. Plus, lists are fun! And you get to use your new notebook!

Unlike other subsets of OCD, like harm OCD or scrupulosity (obsessive guilt about moral or religious issues), ROCD is heavily influenced by the media. A big fear for people with ROCD is whether they're in the "right" relationship—and unfortunately many of us have an unrealistic idea of "right." The media often makes us think that passion needs to be constantly present, and that you should be 100 percent sure you've found your soul mate. While Liza is aware that this type of thinking is a fallacy, she is struggling to unlearn what she's been taught. Rationally, she knows that the idea of "the one" is bullshit, but emotionally, she's having a hard time letting go of the concept. Part of her work in therapy is learning to detach from that ideal and recognize that no relationship is perfect. She's learned that no relationship is going to give you 100 percent of what you want. But if it can give you 80 percent of what you want/ need, you're doing pretty well.

Sheva also has a rather unique view of what a healthy relationship looks like. According to her, unless there is toxicity, pretty much any relationship can work given a certain level of compatibility. When I pushed her on this, asking if you should stay in *any* relationship that *could* work, she pushed back: "Maybe. I think it depends on what you want for your life and what you value. If what's important to you is marrying a provider, there is nothing wrong with that. That is your value system, while another person might place more value on being extremely attracted to their partner. I recommend that people look for higher compatibility in relationships (similar goals for the future, similar lifestyles), but I also recommend people look for *good enough* relationships. The bigger issue is most people seek out and expect perfection in their partners. They often feel like they're settling if they accept anything less, but once you realize perfection is unattainable, it's really not settling at all."

I'm going to be honest: This response blew my mind. The wildest part is that she's absolutely right. In the age of online dating, I've often thought people are far too picky. My peers tend to think the perfect partner is one swipe away—so they keep swiping and swiping until they give up and order Postmates. But I never thought about it in terms of what you value. Some people are going to value stability over passion, and there is absolutely nothing wrong with that. Sheva elaborated on this point by saying, "What you deem a relationship problem and what I deem a relationship problem are different." So while I might not want to marry someone who spends eight hours a week watching football, that might not be an issue for someone else. And I have no grounds to judge them for that. Since there is no such thing as a perfect partner, what's important and doable is figuring out what you specifically need, as well as what you are willing to tolerate.

Not that you asked, but here's my personal breakdown:

- Needs: Kind, trustworthy, funny, attractive to me, smart

- Dealbreakers: Lies, rude, unmotivated, doesn't love dogs

- Can handle: Busy, looks at phone a lot, bad sense of direction, different music taste

- Could happily take but not necessary: Strong, athletic, loves to read, very rich

Take a moment to come up with your own breakdown. I can pretty much guarantee that my breakdown is going to look different than yours. And that's totally fine! In fact, it's good that they're different! What's important is *knowing* your specific breakdown, because it can help you assess if your relationship is, as Sheva puts it, "good enough." Plus, it can help alleviate any anxious thoughts that you're settling or making a "bad choice," because you have a clear idea of what you want and you know whether or not your partner meets that criteria.

———

At this point, we should all have a pretty good understanding of ROCD and some guidelines for how to determine if certain thoughts are ROCD-influenced. Now we have to figure out how to not let ROCD negatively affect romantic relationships. Because that's the good news! It doesn't have to ruin your relationship if you put in the work. And sometimes that work starts as soon as you meet someone new. Sheva says, "For many of my clients, they know something is off when they meet a person who they genuinely like and can see a future with, but their brain begins sending warning signals as if there is a major threat. They start wondering hundreds of times a day, *But do I* really *like them? Are they* really *attractive enough to me?* This dissonance is a dead giveaway that there could be some anxiety at play. It's not that you have to like every person who is good for you, but generally a good person doesn't make a neurotypical brain fire off in quite this way." So that's the first step in the process: recognizing your brain is viewing someone perfectly lovely as a threat and

"Since there is no such thing as a perfect partner, what's important and doable is figuring out what you specifically need, as well as what you are willing to tolerate."

working on it. Ideally you would discuss this in therapy with a professional, but if that's not something you have access to for whatever reason, here are some general tips:

1. Show yourself some goddamn compassion. As Sheva so aptly puts it, "You didn't choose this—it's a mental health condition. It is not your fault. You're not a bad person because you have these doubts. You're not a bad partner or a bad human being because you doubt your relationship. You can only control your behavior. You can't control your thoughts. Being kind to yourself is like lubrication to the whole process." (I cannot stress how much I love the idea of kindness being lubrication for tough situations. Whenever you're struggling, in or out of the bedroom, reach for some lube, baby!)

2. Try to remember that no matter what happens in your relationship, you can cope. You can't control the future and you can't necessarily control your thoughts, but you can cope. If you *have* to think the same thought a hundred times a day, let it be *I can cope*.

3. Do not respond to your anxiety immediately. Take the time to examine it. A useful acronym, according to Sheva, is STOP: Stop, Take a breath, Observe, Proceed. She says, "Oftentimes we're triggered by our partners and react before we even give ourselves a chance to process what's happening. It's very important to slow down and create space between stimulus and response. In that space we have the power to choose a more helpful reaction." She suggests simply going to sleep sometimes, not to avoid your feelings, but to see if you still feel the same way in the morning. (I am almost never still

upset in the morning, which is why I've been known to go to bed at 9:00 p.m. on more than one occasion.)

4 Remember that divorce (or breaking up) is always an option. This might not be the most romantic advice, but Sheva believes it is hugely liberating for people with ROCD. "I think it's very overwhelming for some people to look at marriage as a forever commitment. If they don't even know who they will be tomorrow, how can they know if they'll still want to commit to this relationship in twenty years? It's helpful to remind ourselves that marriage doesn't have to be till-death-do-us-part if one day you no longer want it to be. Reminding ourselves that we have options allows us to relax and, ironically, feel more in love than we might have before," says Sheva. Liza also finds this way of thinking extremely helpful. She's learned it's easier to take her relationship day by day, asking herself, *Do I want to stay* today? Luckily for Brett, her answer has always been yes.

5 Examine your "should" statements. This piece of advice was emphasized repeatedly by both Liza and Sheva. A should statement is anything along the lines of, *We* should *have sex five times a week*; *I* should *only think of my partner when we're intimate*; *I* should *think my partner is gorgeous all of the time*. Aside from avoiding the toxicity we talked about earlier, there are no "shoulds" in a relationship, and acknowledging the fallacy of your "should" statements will help alleviate your anxiety in a big way. I'm not saying you won't still *think* these things, but when they surface, you will know you don't have to listen.

6 Keep your expectations reasonable and not tied to media influence. Don't expect to feel head over heels 100 percent of the time. Don't even expect to be happy with your partner 100 percent of the time. According to Sheva, if you randomly look at your partner and don't find them as attractive as you did in the past, try to remember, "It's Tuesday morning. Who cares? Try again tonight." I personally think we can all use a bit more "who cares" in our daily lives.

This is all work you can do on your own. The tricky part is that a relationship involves (at least) two people. So where does your partner fall into all of this? Should you tell your partner you have ROCD? Like most things in life, the answer is muddy and complicated. Sheva says it's best if they know the basics, such as your OCD or anxiety diagnosis (if you have one). They should also know if you're going to therapy. But it's usually not helpful to get into specifics, especially the content of your worries. Sheva says, "You don't want to give it attention if you recognize it as an OCD thought and it's hurtful. You don't need to tell your partner if you found another person more attractive than them today." Let's all agree to not hurt our partners for no real reason. We only need to share the content of our thoughts if something good can come from it.

For Liza, it was only recently that she finally brought up some of her bigger concerns with Brett. Liza admits they are not great at communicating, so she'd kept a lot of her feelings to herself, both her ROCD thinking and valid issues, out of fear of hurting him. Things had gotten so bad at one point that she was almost ready to break up. But sharing her concerns with him, like their difficulty communicating, ended up bringing them closer because it gave Brett the opportunity to react. "He was really sad. Really emotional. That's something that in a weird way was nice for me to see. I'm so emotional and up and down and I see him as, at least in my head, normal and even. So just seeing any sort of emotional reaction from him was really nice. It evened the playing field a bit, too. And in a fucked up way, it's like, 'Oh, you care about me,'" says Liza.

As you can see from Liza and Brett's experience, there is no clear-cut way to handle ROCD in a relationship, but there are two things you can do to help your partner better understand. The first is letting them know you are actively working on your issues. This can help explain the distance they might be experiencing or any sexual issues you may be having. That way they will know it's not a problem you have with *them*. It's a personal issue, which might make them feel safer in the relationship. The second is actually bringing up the specific issues you've classified as valid and possible to work on together. Otherwise things will snowball without you even giving your partner the opportunity to make the relationship better for both of you.

If you're not currently in a relationship, another piece of this ROCD puzzle is figuring out what *type* of partner you should be looking for. Sheva says she "hates to build a partner," but "for anyone struggling with their mental health, it can be really helpful to find a partner who is patient and understanding. Someone who is able to separate your OCD from the person you actually are. With ROCD, one partner is usually dipping in and out of the relationship emotionally, so it can be quite chaotic for their significant other. Ideally, that partner is someone who can be balanced enough to contain the inconsistency while supporting your growth."

She further breaks down the ideal qualities as:

- Has their own boundaries and can take care of themselves

- Is understanding without allowing you to run over them

- Is not enabling (for example, they don't constantly reassure you or let you voice your ROCD worries all the time)

- Is willing to learn about, understand, and research your condition

- Is emotionally intelligent

- Listens and hears you

Damn! Who wouldn't want a partner like that?! But remember, this is the *ideal*. The MOST important quality and the one you cannot do without is finding a partner who is understanding. Who doesn't dismiss your issues. Who is willing to work on the things that can be worked on. If your current partner simply labels your OCD and/or anxiety as "crazy," now would be a great time to walk away and maybe block their number.

———

Despite having OCD pretty much my entire life, I've rarely suffered from partner-focused ROCD. I've definitely had flickers of ROCD when it comes to my sex life, but most of my mental health issues in regard to my romantic relationships are caused by general anxiety. To get a better understanding of how general anxiety plays a role in our dating lives, I returned to Robin from chapter one.

I started off our call with what I consider to be a very pertinent question: What exactly is anxiety? We all know the term, but do we know what it actually means? According to Robin, "Anxiety is worry or fear that gets expressed through our thoughts (*I'm going to get in trouble, I'm in danger*) or our bodies (butterflies in your stomach, rapid heartbeat, sweating). It can be a powerful indicator of things we need to pay attention to. For example, *I really don't like the feeling of going into my exam unprepared, so next time I'll study harder.* Or, *My heart is pounding as I walk alone down this dark alley, so I should not walk here again at night.* When anxiety is persistent and not related to situations that are truly unhealthy or dangerous, then it becomes problematic." So basically anxiety started out as something to protect us and has evolved into the mortal enemy of pretty much everyone I know. (Raise your hand if you've never experienced unhealthy anxiety. Wow! You're a unicorn.)

The fact that there is good anxiety and unhealthy anxiety brings up the same difficulties as ROCD. How can you tell the difference? Luckily, Robin was able to break anxiety surrounding romantic relationships into three separate types:

1 **General anxiety that bleeds into the relationship.**
Someone with general anxiety feels anxious in many other parts of their life, so it makes sense they would also feel anxious when it comes to relationships. It's simply how their brain works and is not necessarily based on specific external situations.

2 **Anxiety specific to intimacy.** Robin says, "Sometimes anxiety in relationships is related to what we call attachment disorders. Our first relationships are with our primary

caregivers. If they have their own emotional difficulties, they may not be able to provide the kind of reliable and constant responses that young children need. For example, instead of picking up the child over and over again when they reach out their arms or responding routinely to the baby's cries for comfort and caretaking, the parent gets annoyed by the child's demands or simply spaces out. The child can become overanxious about the whereabouts of their caregivers or have excessive difficulties separating from them. The child grows up unable to feel secure in romantic relationships, not because of what's going on in the current relationship, but because of their history of not being able to count on their caregivers. This becomes an unconscious template for how all relationships are expected to go." To summarize, someone with intimacy anxiety might travel through life relatively calm, but once they get romantically close to someone, their brain starts to freak out due to past experiences. The good news is this is something you can absolutely work on. The bad news is people rarely identify that this is the cause of how they're feeling. It might be helpful to look into your attachment style if this pattern of anxiety feels familiar to you.

3 **Helpful anxiety.** Or what Robin calls "your wisdom." This type of anxiety flares up when "there is a part of you that knows this is not good and safe, and another part that keeps making excuses. *He doesn't return my calls because he's so busy.* Or, *He's just friendly and that's why he's talking to all these other girls.* All those ways we talk ourselves out of knowing what we know." THIS is the anxiety you want to listen to. Learn to quiet yourself down and take the time

to listen to your wisdom. You can then act accordingly by getting yourself out of that unsafe situation/relationship.

For the rest of this chapter we will focus on the unhealthy types of relationship anxiety (i.e., types one and two), but I want to quickly address anxiety number three. I love that Robin calls this anxiety your wisdom because that's exactly what it is. So many times I've been in the wrong relationship but tried to tell myself I was just feeling anxious because I'm an anxious person. In reality, I should have listened to what my wisdom was trying to tell me. I would like to take a moment to personally thank my wisdom and apologize for blowing it off so many times: I need you, I love you, and I promise to listen to you to the best of my ability from now on.

You can all take a moment to address your wisdom as well. I'll wait.

(Hold for wisdom-thanking.)

And we're back! Missed you!

When it comes to unhealthy anxiety, the biggest takeaway is that it is your job, not your partner's, to learn how to soothe it. Robin explains, "People sometimes feel like they should be looking to their partner for reassurance, repeatedly. The part of you that can't settle down really belongs to you to soothe. And your partner is like your secondary helper. In other words, a good partner is communicative and stays in touch and is affectionate and loving. That is just the job of a good, loving partner. And the job of the anxious person is to see that and be able to separate a little bit from the scared part that is ruminating or obsessing. And to be able to talk to that part, to have these conversations with that scared part: *I know you're really anxious now, and I know this feels really bad. I feel like we're okay here. I feel like right here, right now—this is good. I can see him. He's a loving person. I feel cared about by him. I feel respected.* And this is going to sound weird, but listen to that part's concerns. Is your scared part concerned about the what-ifs? What if *he grows tired of me?* What if *he finds somebody else?* The job of the wise adult is to say, *Look—you know I don't know what the future holds in any respect. Right here, right now, which is all we know, this feels good. I think this is safe.*

Robin isn't telling you to dismiss your anxiety or shove it to the back of your mind. She's suggesting you engage it in a healthy discussion. Get to know the specific anxiety so you know how to tackle it. Just like with ROCD, an easy way to see if your anxiety is valid or harmful is to examine the content of the anxiety. Is it based on something that is actually happening, or is it future-based? If it's not based on the present, you're simply fortune-telling and catastrophizing. In those cases, as Robin puts it, it's important to remind your anxiety that "these are just stories you're making up. You could believe them, but it's going to cost you." I can attest that I've wasted far too many nights worrying about something my brain conjured out of nothing. I think we can all agree anxiety is exhausting and not in a fun way that puts you right to sleep. (Pretty unfair, if you ask me!)

Another great way to tackle anxiety is to gain some perspective. Robin says that while in the midst of your anxiety, "you are so overcome with feelings that it can be really helpful to take a step back and look at it as if it was happening to somebody else." Would you be as worried if a friend brought up the same concerns you're dealing with? Probably not. You might even think they were over-reacting. Try to view the situation as an objective outsider as much as you can.

Robin also does a lot of body work with her patients to combat anxiety. She was kind enough to break down what that entails:

1. Locate where your anxiety exists in your body. It might be in your stomach, in your heart, in your head. (I personally feel it in my chest.) Put your hand over where you feel the anxiety.

2. Put your feet on the ground and "actually use the muscles in your feet to feel how solid it is. Then lengthen your spine, because shifting your posture is very powerful."

3. Take some time to look around the room or whatever space you're in and engage in some grounding self-talk.

Robin explains that what you're trying to do through these three physical steps is reactivate a part of your brain that can shut down when you're overwhelmed. You want to turn that bit back on "because that's the part of your brain that's a much better problem-solver than panic or anxiety, which are not good problem-solvers at all." You're basically activating a more grounded sense of self to overpower the intense feelings of anxiety. Robin says the goal is "putting your hand where the anxiety is in that moment in your body, like your stomach, looking around so you can be present in this moment, and talking to these different parts of yourself from the perspective of the grounded part of you." Because the grounded part of you exists. The trick is learning how to access it at all times, even in moments of extreme distress.

This is work you have to tackle on your own. If you have anxiety specifically related to intimacy, you might also want to unpack your past with a therapist and get to the root of the issue. But let's assume you're doing the work and trying your best to get your anxiety under control. How do you go about dating in the meantime? Twenty-five-year-old me had absolutely no idea! For most of my twenties, I was brimming with so much anxiety, I'm surprised I didn't burst. I had no idea how to talk myself down from the ledge, and I relied on unhealthy behaviors to self-soothe, such as checking my then-boyfriend's activity on Instagram multiple times a day. (Man, did he like a lot of other women's pictures.) Since then, I'm much less anxious in general and was actually able to feel safe in my most recent relationship.

When I interviewed Robin for this book, I was still in said relationship and had noticed that while my overall anxiety was down, I would still get irrationally worried if I couldn't immediately get in touch with my partner. I shared this fear with him, and he agreed to let me know ahead of time if he was going to be away from his phone for a few hours. I mentioned this agreement to Robin and wondered if I was asking him to enable my anxiety. Much to my delight, she said no! In fact, she found the request quite healthy: "That's the idea of being a secondary helper. You don't say 'Fuck you. That's your problem.' Partners are always accommodating to each other. If he's cool with that, that's great. He's not going to be perfect, but it makes sense that that would be a great accommodation."

While what I asked for was acceptable, Robin said it is possible to go about the same request the wrong way: "It's not about being too anxious. It's about expecting the other person to be in charge of your anxiety. It's one thing to say, 'Gee, when I don't hear from you, I get scared,' versus 'There's something wrong with you

> "We all want to be heard. We all want to be understood. We don't want to be judged for things out of our control. And we want to feel safe. We just have to remember that all of this takes work."

that I couldn't reach you for two hours. You're a jerk!'" It's vital to remember that you are the one accountable for your anxiety, not your partner. I've been dealing with this long enough that I know my triggers and have learned to express them. But if my future partner happens to get stuck in an unexpectedly long meeting and I can't reach him, it's *my* job to sit with the discomfort. And I will do that by locating the anxiety in my body, using the muscles in my feet to feel the solidness of the floor, looking around the room to ground myself in the moment, and accessing the part of my brain that is smart enough to realize: It's 3:00 p.m. on a Tuesday. He's probably in a freaking meeting!

Robin shares a similar point of view with Sheva when it comes to finding a compatible partner if you struggle with relationship anxiety. She says you need someone who will be accommodating, but then she pointed out that *everyone* should look for someone accommodating. A lot of what makes someone a good partner for a person with anxiety or ROCD is simply what makes someone a good partner in general. We all want to be heard. We all want to be understood. We don't want to be judged for things out of our control. And we want to feel safe. We just have to remember that all of this takes work.

As Sheva so brilliantly put it, "Love is really a verb. It's an action. We have to remember it's not just a feeling. It doesn't just happen to you. Infatuation happens to you. And lust happens to you. And even chemistry, to some extent, happens to you. But really working on a long-term relationship and building something with someone doesn't just happen. That's a garden and you have to be in there. You can't just be like, 'My garden is dying. Why?'" But if you're willing to put in the work with yourself and your relationship, your hydrangea will be one hundred feet tall in no time! (I know nothing about gardening, but you get the idea.)

———

After much deliberation, here are my top takeaways from talking to Sheva and Robin:

- ROCD is different from normal doubts. It's incessant and often has negative effects on romantic relationships. It's important to figure out if you have ROCD so you can start to recognize these harmful thought patterns.

- ROCD can be heavily influenced by the media. The main fear surrounding ROCD is wondering if this is the "right" relationship, and, unfortunately, many of us have an unrealistic idea of "right."

- Share your diagnosis with your partner, but don't unnecessarily tell them the content of your worries if they're not things they can change.

- It is *your* job to soothe your anxiety. Your partner is simply a secondary helper.

- What you deem a relationship problem and what I deem a relationship problem are different. You need to figure out what *you* value and what you're willing to tolerate.

- Use body work to help activate the grounded part of your brain so it can talk to your anxiety.

- There is such a thing as helpful anxiety. It's your wisdom. (And you should thank it!)

- Look for a partner who is understanding and accommodating without enabling you.

- Do not respond to your anxiety immediately. Take the time to examine it. STOP: Stop, Take a breath, Observe, Proceed.

- Show yourself some goddamn compassion. (Kindness = lube.)

Wow! We have already learned so much—and even used lube as a metaphor! If that's not motivation to keep reading, I don't know what is!

CHAPTER THREE

HOW DO I AVOID AN UNHEALTHY RELATIONSHIP?

MEET THE EXPERTS:

- **Dr. Annette Rotter, PhD,** has been a practicing clinical psychologist in Westchester and New York City for more than twenty-five years. Her private practice includes work with couples, adults, adolescents, and divorcing parents. Annette especially loves helping couples improve their connection, find positive strategies to understand each other better, and resolve conflicts with greater ease. She also has extensive clinical experience working with families in crisis and teaching parents the skills to reduce conflict and address the developmental needs of their children. Annette earned her BA in American Studies from Brown University and her PhD with distinction in Clinical Psychology from Yeshiva University. We'll be referring to her as Annette.

- **Dr. Zac Seidler** is a clinical psychologist, the director of Mental Health Training at Movember, and a research fellow with Orygen at the University of Melbourne. Zac has devoted several years to the goal of reducing the staggering male suicide rate by treating and researching men's mental health. Zac has worked clinically with men of different ages and presentations, from adolescents with early psychosis to older HIV+ men struggling with adjustment. Currently, Zac is trialing the world's first online program, Men in Mind, to train mental health clinicians in how to better understand and respond to men's distress. We'll be referring to him as Zac.

For years and years and years, I was a nightmare to date. I would punish my partners if I felt ignored by them. I would question and attack their friendships with other women. I would force the relationship along at a pace that made my partner feel uneasy. And then, when the relationship would inevitably end, I would get into a new one as quickly as possible to repeat the cycle. You might be wondering, along with most of my exes, how I can have the audacity to write a book about healthy relationships when this is my history. But I think it is only through having this embarrassing history that I'm better able to identify what behaviors can corrupt a relationship and what changes I needed to make in order to find happiness with another person. You might be super surprised, given the premise of this book, but I'm pretty sure the majority of my past issues stemmed from my unsteady mental health and an inability to properly regulate my emotions. Huge reveal, right?!

That said, I was not always the sole culprit in my many failed relationships. There were times when my partner exacerbated my bad behavior and/or was the main source of the bad behavior. So I know what it's like both to sabotage my relationship and watch someone else self-sabotage. In this chapter, I'm going to explore two specific relationships. In one, my inability to address my failing mental health led to our breakup. In the other, my partner's inability to address his failing mental health helped cause the same outcome. My goal is that by examining my past, you will be encouraged to do the same. It is only through introspection that we are able to properly identify our harmful habits and patterns. (Unless you have a really nosy best friend who likes to point these things out.) I am living proof that it's possible to break the cycle and change how you act and, often even more importantly, react. And once you change your behavior, you might also be able to change your thoughts and feelings for the better. For example, you might not have to *pretend* to be okay with your partner's new hot coworker because you actually *are* okay with it as a result of being secure in yourself and your relationship! How cool is that?! The American Dream! (Or at least my version of it!)

―――

Here's a tricky one: How do you know if you're in the wrong relationship? Unless there is clear abuse, it's often difficult to identify an unhealthy relationship, so I asked psychologist Dr. Annette Rotter to help us pinpoint the signs. Even as a professional couple's therapist with more than twenty-five years of experience, she admitted it is hard to succinctly define: "I would say if people are struggling and in conflict more often than they're feeling comforted, stronger, and better because of the relationship, that would be a signal of an unhealthy relationship. Are you able to pursue the things that you're interested in? Are you supported in those things? Is the person overly critical or dictating too much in the relationship? Is it collaborative? In healthy relationships it's not that there's no conflict or struggle; it's more that there's a sense of learning how to recover from conflict and growing closer to each other as you navigate struggles."

One of the big shifts that occurred in my last relationship was deciding to never view my partner as my adversary. Instead, I was determined to always be on the same team. Entering into every fight or disagreement you have with your partner with this mindset can completely change the outcome for the better. Why? You can't win by defeating the other person when you are on the same team. So instead of attacking, you have to come to a solution that works for both of you. Even if that sometimes means one person admitting the other is right. But since you're on the same team, you both get the win! Way to go!

I strongly believe that one of the best ways to figure out if you are in an unhealthy relationship or about to enter into one is by taking the time to examine your mental state. There have been times in my life where no matter how wonderful the other person was, I simply wasn't stable enough for a true partnership. Annette agrees that sometimes you're simply not in the right place to date: "If one person is struggling so much that they can't make space for the other person's needs, and they are so preoccupied or underwater that they are taking more than giving, that's not a great way to start a relationship." It's different, of course, if you are already in a relationship and then go through a tough time. "When you are in a relationship, there are going to be things that will be challenging for any couple: unemployment, illness, loss. If you have a shared history wherein you were both healthy enough to be supportive of each other and there was a mutuality in terms of giving and receiving, that can help sustain you during those periods when somebody's having a bumpy time, because you are able to reflect back to a time when it felt very different," says Annette.

In other words, it's a lot more reasonable to ask someone to weather a storm with you when you already have a strong foundation. That way, you know you're both capable of having a healthy and mutual partnership, even if one person is currently going through a rocky patch. But if either of you are barreling into a new relationship with thunder and lightning licking at your heels, it might be best to walk away before it turns into a hurricane. The early stages of relationships often establish what become your long-term dynamics. Annette explains, "If there are couples who came together when one of the two was struggling in a way that was so massive and the other person was playing more of a total support and rescue role, the relationship is structured in an imbalanced way from the beginning." So if your ultimate goal is an equal partnership, I would suggest only entering into relationships when you have the mental capacity to give as much as you receive in order to establish a strong foundation and healthy dynamics.

Now, if you're someone like me who has struggled on and off with your mental health for a long time, it might be difficult to decipher when you're in a good enough place to date and when you're not. The expectation here isn't, *I'm completely perfect and I never do anything wrong and therefore I deserve a partner*. Instead, Annette says, "It's about how all-consuming your personal struggle is. If the balance is so far off that you're having trouble just navigating the world individually without that partner, if you can't find any satisfaction and meaning just being in the world on your own, again, you are probably not coming from a healthy enough place to enter into a relationship. Anxiety can be all-consuming. Depression can be all-consuming. I think when you're in it you know what it feels like to be swallowed up by it. If you're think-ing you really should be getting help but you're not getting it, you should probably get the help first. Take that step first rather than looking for a relationship."

Annette says you can also use your own history as a guide to help you make an informed decision: "Have you felt this way before? What were you like in your [previous] relationships when you felt like this?" Maybe you've been okay dating in the past despite periods of high anxiety, or maybe your history suggests it would be better to take a break until you get back to baseline. According to Annette, it's also helpful to look at all aspects of your life before diving into the dating pool: "Is your anxiety dominating your rela-tionships with your friends? What's your functioning like at work? What's your functioning like in your family? What would they all say about how you seem? I think if you are struggling across the board, it's likely an inadvisable time to start a relationship." My first reaction to the hypothetical situation of asking my friends and family if I'm in a good enough place to date is pure terror. How dare they say what I should or should not do! But the more I sat with the idea, the more I saw its merit. As long as you're only asking people who have your best interests at heart and truly know you, there is no harm in getting their opinion, especially since it might turn into encouragement to get back out there.

I know what some of you might be thinking. You're depressed because you are single. Your anxiety will go away as soon as you don't have to worry about finding a life partner anymore. I often felt the same thing. And to some degree, I think this is true. My last rela-tionship helped me grow and reach more of my potential because I wasn't fixated on being alone all the time. I had the mental energy to focus on other things. My brain now knows how to operate in a new, more productive way due to that experience. Not to be overly mushy, but being securely loved can function as a proverbial sigh of relief. Unfortunately, this added comfort isn't something you can feel or even access if you're currently drowning. Think of it this way: Your potential partner is an outstretched hand that can help bring you to shore. But you can only reach out and successfully grab this hand if you're already almost on land. If you're thirty feet out, your partner can't help you, even if you both really want them to be able to. No one's arms are that long, even if your partner is very good-looking and tall. You've got to get twenty-eight feet closer on your own (and/or with the help of mental health professionals/medication/psychoeducation/meditation/coping skills/mindfulness—you get it!). Only then can the help they are offering actually reach you and make a difference.

———

One of my biggest issues with a guy we are going to call Dylan is that while I respected the shit out of him, I didn't view myself as his equal. And when it comes to a healthy relationship, respect not only has to flow both ways between partners, it also has to apply to how each person feels about themselves. When we started dating in 2016, I thought, without a doubt, that Dylan was out of my league. This might not seem like that big of an issue, but if you go into a partnership feeling inferior, it is going to negatively impact every corner of your relationship. My reasons for feeling unworthy were mainly leftover insecurities from growing up. I still saw myself as an outsider/weirdo who people might tolerate for a bit before growing sick of me. Dylan, on the other hand, was not only extremely handsome, but he lived in a house with four other guys who partied like they were still in college. At twenty-seven, I found this intimidatingly cool. (Now that I'm in my thirties, I simply find it unseemly.) The first time I went to his house was on the Fourth of July, and they had a bunch of attractive people over doing attractive things. As he introduced me around, I assumed everyone was thinking the same thing: *What the hell is he doing with her?!* In reality, people probably weren't thinking of me at all. Not in a bad way, but simply in a "we are all the stars of our own stories" sort of way. (Realizing just how little other people think about you is unbelievably liberating IMHO!)

Throughout our ten-month relationship, I obsessed over keeping Dylan. I would sit in my therapist's office and lament that if we ever broke up, I wouldn't be able to console myself since this was the first guy I had dated who didn't have flaws. In every other relationship, there was always some way to spin it so that I'd be better off without him. I could not see a scenario where I would be better off without Dylan, since Dylan was perfect. Was Dylan actually perfect? Of course not. But I had put him on a pedestal, much to my own detriment.

Here are some signs that you have put your partner on a pedestal:

1. Constantly thinking, *I don't deserve this person.*

2. Constantly thinking, *People probably think we are a mismatched couple.*

3. Constantly thinking, *Wow! How did I trick this person into loving me?!*

4. Occasionally thinking, *Maybe my partner is the lucky one? Nah! I'm a piece of shit!*

It makes sense that if your brain has been telling you horrible things about yourself for years, you're going to believe some, if not all, of them. Plus, self-stigma is a real, prevalent thing. You could be the most famous mental health advocate in the world and still privately judge yourself for your disorder. So the idea that someone with this sort of painful history could start dating a person who would never have looked twice at them in high school and *not* feel inferior in some way is unlikely. The only way to avoid this is to reach a level of self-confidence and self-acceptance that is hard to come by without putting in a lot of work.

I hadn't yet completed this work when I started seeing Dylan. I was still too attached to a younger version of me, who suffered rejection after rejection. Despite being somewhat internet famous and successful, my self-image hadn't caught up to the person I had become. I promised myself when I started working on this book that I wouldn't rely on the old adage "You have to love yourself before someone else can love you" because you've already heard it a million times and I also don't think it's true. Plenty of people are loved even when they don't love themselves. The issue is whether you're able to have a healthy and sustainable love that is satisfying for both partners without *also* loving yourself. That scenario is much harder to find.

The least helpful thing I could do here is tell you all to put in the "work" to love yourself and then not define what that actually means. When I mention "work," I'm primarily talking about eliminating negative self-talk, reconstructing personal schemas, and reframing how you look at things. There were plenty of times with my most recent partner when I briefly wondered what he got out of our relationship (old habits die hard). The big difference is that when I would ask myself the same question during my relationship with Dylan, I didn't have an answer. Now, instead of doubling down on this fear that I am unworthy, I am able to think about all the things I do bring to the table. (I won't list them all here, but I will mention I am very good at silly dancing. And whatever comes to your mind when I mention "silly dancing" is correct.)

It's also important to consciously shift away from the idea that you can rank someone's value in this world. If you make your partner happy and they make you happy, then you are perfectly matched, regardless of who makes more money or has better muscle definition.

I find it exciting and encouraging that all of these small, day-to-day changes in our thoughts can influence larger changes in our personal schemas. Think of schemas as the lenses through which we view the world. If my personal schema says I'm unlovable or unworthy of happiness, I will see everyone's behavior through that lens. It won't matter if someone actually does love me because my brain won't allow me to process their affection correctly. That's why self-awareness is so important. It enables you to properly identify any schemas that aren't serving you. For example, I used to firmly believe that my value as a person was directly tied to my work productivity. If I wasn't being productive, I wasn't worth anything. Or to put it more clearly, I was a "waste of space" while everyone else was out saving lives and making millions. I think we can all agree my work schema was (1) incorrect, and (2) actively hurting me.

When I first started dating Dylan, I had a lot going on professionally. I was working a few days a week on a sketch show for a now-defunct app. I was cowriting my first novel. I had a pilot in development at FX. Toward the end of our relationship, I had quit the sketch show, finished writing the book, and my pilot was dead in the water. I was bored out of my mind with no new projects on the horizon. This was when my harmful work/productivity schema started to bleed into my relationship. The only thing my anxiety enjoys feeding off more than uncertainty is boredom. So instead of spending my days relishing my lack of responsibility, I became fixated on having nothing to do. Guilt and shame consumed me. My self-hatred began to eat away at my mental health, and I found myself crying constantly and not knowing what to do with my life.

Let's take a step back for a moment and look at the bigger picture, shall we? What exactly was causing me to spin out of control? Was I in financial trouble? Nope. I had made enough money off those other projects to be more than fine for quite a while. Was my career completely over? Also nope. I was months away from having my first book come out, and it would eventually be a *New York Times* bestseller. (Only for one week, but who cares? I get to say that for the rest of my life!) Was I truly a lazy, disgusting piece of human garbage who didn't contribute one positive thing to the world? I'll let you guess the answer to that one. So why did I go over to Dylan's house one night, on the verge of tears, and proclaim, "I'm not happy"? The answer is surprisingly simple: I was working off of an unhealthy and fictitious point of view that desperately needed reframing.

When I dramatically proclaimed "I'm not happy" in Dylan's doorway, I meant I wasn't happy in my day-to-day life/career. But Dylan immediately assumed I was talking about our relationship. And why wouldn't he? When someone is so profoundly miserable, it's almost impossible for their partner not to take it personally. So what's the right move? Is it the responsibility of the person who is suffering to walk away from the relationship if they can see they're bringing their partner down with them?

Annette says it's not so clear-cut: "To put this into a physical paradigm, if you found out you had a terminal illness, is it your responsibility to walk away from the relationship? In a way, that leaves the other person out. They might not want you to walk away from the relationship. If you recognize that your problem is affecting the relationship badly, that's a discussion to have: 'I think my anxiety is casting a shadow over the way that we connect and it's destructive.' And you might decide you shouldn't be in the relationship, but you decide it together." So while it's not on the unwell person to unilaterally leave the relationship, it *is* their responsibility to acknowledge what is going on and initiate a discussion about it.

Did I initiate such a discussion with Dylan? Kind of but not really. We definitely acknowledged and analyzed my personal struggle and I'm sure I made some sort of vow to work on myself. But I never asked him about his experience dating me *and* my anxiety. His internal monologue was a mystery to me that I never bothered to solve. That's why it came as such a shock when he sat me down one afternoon and told me that my anxiety had been affecting him in a big (negative) way. I, in turn, handled his confession horribly. Instead of listening to what he was saying, the moment he mentioned the word "anxiety," I went on the defensive. After years of living with mental illness and making immense (if not enough) progress, I was *enraged* that my boyfriend had the audacity to complain about it. I could feel the anger coursing through my veins. Instead of absorbing what he was saying, I was plotting ways to enact my revenge through psychological warfare so I could hurt him as much as he had just hurt me. This was clearly a super grounded and healthy response. (JK.)

Toward the end of our terse conversation, Dylan asked if he could give me a hug. I refused in an effort to punish him, and we proceeded to go to a friend's party, where I pretended everything was fine because I was immature and enjoyed mind games. For months after we eventually broke up, I wondered what would have happened if I'd let him hug me in that moment instead of refusing out of spite. *Would we still be together? Would my life be perfect? Did I destroy my one chance at love and happiness by being a petty little bitch?* Talk about ruminating, am I right?! But the past is the past. And the night following the hug that never was, we went to see a movie, where I gave him the cold shoulder. It was a childish response and I don't know what I planned to get out of it. Maybe some proclamation of love and regret? Well, that never came. Instead, neither of us mentioned my bad mood until I dropped him off later that night and he closed my car door loudly. This simple act of frustration caused me to spiral because I was convinced that *he* was now the one mad at *me* and I was no longer the clear "victim" in the situation. I panicked as I watched all my "power" from being the wronged party seep away.

That's the problem with constantly monitoring the power dynamic in your relationship: Even when you think you're winning, you've already lost by playing the game in the first place. Happy people don't worry about this stuff. Healthy relationships don't revolve around mind games. I was invested in a war where my opponent was the person I loved, and he hadn't even signed up to fight, let alone go into battle. And yet, somehow, I had managed to defeat myself within twenty-four hours. About an hour after the car door "slam," I called him sobbing on the phone, begging for forgiveness as my dog looked on, disgusted by my theatrics.

For a long time, I didn't have the right vocabulary to describe how my brain worked. I thought I was just overly emotional. Volatile. I lived in fear of my own reactions. My parents would tiptoe around me, worried something would set me off. I walked, ran, and sat around worried about the same thing. It wasn't until I started a master's program in clinical psychology at age thirty that I first heard and fully processed the term "emotional regulation." I learned that one of the most common objectives in therapy is to help the client learn how to regulate their emotions. Learning how to regulate mine over the last few years, without even realizing that was my goal, has been a game changer. Instead of immediately responding with intense, overpowering emotion, I'm now able to take in information, evaluate it, and consider the appropriate response. That doesn't mean I don't get angry or frustrated. It just means that when I do get angry or frustrated, those feelings don't consume me. I'm able to remain levelheaded while still experiencing and acknowledging my emotions. This prevents me from lashing out or staying stuck in a bad place for longer than necessary.

None of this was true when I was with Dylan. As a result, I panicked following our failed movie night, still triggered by our earlier conversation and evidence of what I perceived to be him pulling away. Dylan assured me over the phone that he wasn't breaking up with me. If he did that, he would be an asshole. Instead, he was just sharing his feelings so our relationship could improve. This happened on a Monday. He dumped me that Wednesday. I have not seen him since.

Up until fairly recently, I painted Dylan as a villain. Even as I longed for a reconciliation, I licked my wounds by trashing him to every single person who would listen. My perceived version of events was simple: We were in a great relationship, I started to go through a tough time with my mental health, he promised not to leave me because of it, and then two days later he was gone. I was being punished for having a mental illness and he was the devil incarnate.

In reality, I had failed to address my deteriorating mental state in a timely manner and then lashed out at him for trying to talk about it. There were other, bigger issues, too, like our different lifestyles and the fact that he thought if we got married it would ultimately end in divorce. (What a fun thing to learn while someone is dumping you!) We were incompatible in many, many ways, even if I got off on posting pictures of his gorgeous bone structure on my Instagram. But directly following the breakup, I was unable to see all of this and instead wanted, very badly, to die. This breakup brought me to such a dark place that I ultimately went back on medication for the first time in years. (For more on psychotropics, refer to chapter five!)

At the time, I didn't think my relationship with Dylan started out unhealthy in terms of our dynamic with each other. For most of our relationship, I felt I had finally gotten it right. But there were cracks in the foundation, and as soon as there was outside pressure—this time in the form of my career insecurity, unaddressed inferiority complex, and immature game-playing—the entire structure began to crack. Did the whole thing have to crumble to the ground as a result? Of course not. But at that point I wasn't able to properly address the underlying issues in my own life, and Dylan didn't view our relationship as something worth fighting for. When things got tough, he found it easier to leave. I hate to say it, but there is actually nothing wrong with that. We weren't married. We didn't have children together. And even if those things were true, you're always allowed to break up.

Obviously, when talking about all of this, we have to take into account the seriousness and longevity of the relationship. It's very different to walk away after three months versus twenty years and two children. But, as mentioned earlier, this book is primarily focused on new relationships and relationships that are only a few years old. It's during the period without a marriage license, without children, without a shared mortgage that you should really take your time to assess if this is the dynamic you want long term. And, as Annette says, "If a new relationship needs all that heavy lifting, and that's what it feels like—like lifting a two-ton truck—it's probably not a great start. It shouldn't have to feel that hard." Did you hear that? Relationships don't have to be a near-constant battle for there to be true passion and love! Who knew! (I guess pretty much every mental health professional . . .)

I completely understand where our instilled belief that "true" love should be hard comes from. You don't need to look any further than whatever program is currently on your TV. It makes for a better narrative when someone has to jump through fiery hoops and disown their family in order to be with their one and only. The problem is that these stories are always framed as romantic instead of unhealthy and/or traumatizing. As a writer, I get that it's hard to make a compelling movie about two people who meet at a house party, share similar interests, get married, live another fifty years in harmony, and then die. But real life doesn't need to be dramatic to be enjoyable. I personally don't think it's dull to eat lunch with the same person day after day. I think if you can do that successfully, and still love that person even after you've grown completely sick of sandwiches, you've accomplished something tremendous with your life.

In the spirit of nurturing healthy connections and finding someone to eat lunch with you, I think it's important for anyone with a history of mental health issues to only date partners who validate those experiences. Annette elaborates on this point: "If you've been in therapy and on medication at times, that is probably something that will come up again. And if you enter into a relationship with a partner who doesn't appreciate or get that, who sees psychology or psychiatry or any kind of mental health issue as weakness or doesn't believe in therapy, you're really setting yourself up in, I think, a dangerous way. Because ideally, you want to seek out someone who is enlightened and brings to the table things you value.

"You deserve to be with someone who respects you enough to also respect your distress, even if they don't understand it."

Hopefully, you are engaging with someone who is open-minded, even if they're not a therapy [expert]." This is perhaps the most clear-cut way to determine if you've just entered or are about to enter into an unhealthy relationship. If you get the sense they don't believe in therapy or the importance of mental health, abort before you even order dessert. Or maybe order dessert to go if there are some great options, like a fruit tart.

Another thing to look out for is how your partner treats your specific symptoms, even if they seem accepting of the *idea* of mental health challenges. We've all been around people who roll their eyes when we're visibly struggling. While it can be hard for people to understand the ins and outs of mental illness if they're neurotypical, you deserve to be with someone who respects you enough to also respect your distress, even if they don't understand it. On top of that, the relationship will fare much better if your partner is able to successfully listen and take in what will and will not help you. Annette says, "Generally when someone is anxious, it is not super helpful to say 'just relax.' Saying 'you're being crazy' never works. If you have data from your past about what is comforting, that is very helpful to share with your partner. If they're on your side, if you trust them, you can say, 'I know you're trying to be helpful to me by telling me to check my OCD at the door, but that approach is making it worse and it would be so helpful if you X, Y, or Z.' If they don't want to be empathic or they don't have the capacity to be empathic, they're probably not the right partner and that's not a bad thing to find out sooner than later."

For many, your life partner is the person you are going to spend the most time with out of everyone on planet Earth. Their disposition, personality, and actions are going to greatly influence the life you live, what your day-to-day looks like, where you go, and how you get there. That's why it's so important that the core of your relationship be healthy and full of mutual respect. And that piece is something that needs to be established right away, even if all the other stuff—love, commitment, sexual satisfaction—needs more time to grow. Make sure you take the time when getting to know someone to assess if that crucial foundation is possible, and then go one step further: Is this person capable of building that with someone else right now?

You might be thinking it's hard enough to decipher your own internal workings—how can I possibly ask you to decipher someone else's and determine if they are fit to date? Luckily, I'm not asking you to do that! In no way, shape, or form is it your place or responsibility to diagnose or label your (potential) partner in any pathological way. Instead, when you are getting to know someone, I would simply encourage you to look for signs that they are capable of forming a healthy relationship. Do they have an active social life filled with meaningful friendships, or have they have been staying home and isolating? When you don't reply to their text right away, do they immediately double text, anxious to get a reply? If you have to cancel plans at the last minute, are they understanding, or are they angry? Are they using alcohol or drugs as a means to cope? I once started dating someone who was in the throes of a depressive episode. Within two months, we were breaking up while I was simultaneously encouraging him to get help. I spent the next few days doing unofficial welfare checks on him while also licking my own wounds of rejection. Imagine constantly contacting someone who just broke up with you because you are afraid they might hurt themselves. It was not fun! And it was something that could have been avoided if I did a better job of listening to what he was telling me about himself and his current situation from the beginning.

Unfortunately, things aren't always so clear-cut. Even if someone is in a bad place when you first meet, they might momentarily feel a lot better with the rush of a new romance, only for their mental health to dramatically go south once the honeymoon phase is over. Other times, your new partner's mental health might start off okay but fall apart slowly over time as they continuously resist help. My failed relationship with a guy we are going to call Max had aspects of both of those scenarios, plus a few glaring red flags at the beginning that I ignored.

I met Max two months after my devastating breakup with Dylan. You read that right! Only two months after my suicidal ideation was so strong that I had to go on medication, I was throwing myself back on the horse and galloping along without a saddle. (Horse experts will know this is *very* dangerous. I once broke the growth plate in my arm after falling off a horse without a saddle, and he was only trotting, which is much slower than galloping.) Before my first Bumble date with Max, I got violently sick and had to sit on the toilet right up until I called my Uber. Was this my body's way of telling me I wasn't ready to date again? Probably! Did I listen? No way! I had already picked out a cute outfit. It even showed a little bit of my midriff! There was no turning back, diarrhea be damned.

My first date with Max was, to put it lightly, a disaster. He was so nervous we barely spoke, and I felt uncomfortable the whole time. This was confusing since our text banter had been off the charts. I chalked it up to nerves and gave him a second chance. I was so determined to find my person and not be alone that I was willing to overlook, well, everything. We then proceeded to date for an entire year until his mental health got so out of control that I had to break up with him in his therapist's office. (Remember that fun anecdote from chapter two?! *Memories* . . . make me reevaluate all of my decision-making.) I quickly learned the "nerves" I so casually disregarded on our first date were actually overwhelming social anxiety. Obviously, there is nothing wrong with having social anxiety. Millions of people have it (it's one of the most common anxiety disorders), and they are just as deserving and capable of love and happiness as anyone else. The problem was that Max was not dealing with any of his issues, which included alcohol use as an unhealthy coping mechanism, and this started to negatively affect our relationship. How could it not?!

While Max had been seeing a therapist before we met, she went on maternity leave at the time we started dating, so he was no longer in treatment. For about ten months I encouraged him to find a new therapist. For about ten months he didn't. I asked Annette if it's even kosher to suggest your partner see a therapist and she said, "Absolutely! I don't see suggesting that you're worried about someone or saying that you're hoping they'll get help for themselves as critical or negative. Offering or suggesting or wishing that your partner will get some help when they're suffering is actually a loving thing to do." Okay, great! I did the right thing! The problem was that it didn't lead to change. Max would go back and forth on agreeing that he needed to see someone, but ultimately, he didn't take action until we were already on the verge of breaking up and his old therapist was back from maternity leave.

This kind of interaction appears in all areas of life. You suggest something that might improve someone's happiness, be it exercise, therapy, or even acupuncture. They agree but then do nothing. When you bring it back up, they agree again, yet still do nothing. How do you argue with someone who is agreeing with you? It's impossible! Annette acknowledged that when your partner is being resistant, you're in for more than one tough interaction: "If you are involved with someone who seems to be really troubled and they're not willing to get the help, that's usually more than one conversation. If you really care about someone, say, 'I'm getting more concerned. It's hard for me to be with somebody who isn't willing to take the steps to take care of themselves.' The person who is saying the other has a problem without seeing it acted upon is going to grow increasingly unhappy. It's not going to be resolved." And that lack of resolution might just wear down your relationship until there's nothing left to fight for. I remember thinking toward the end of my relationship with Max, *What am I even getting out of this anymore?!* The affection and attention I was initially wooed by had turned into judgment and moodiness as his mental state deteriorated. I could feel him growing increasingly resentful of me. This all caused me to grieve the end of that relationship while I was still in it, and by the time it was officially over, I felt a huge sense of relief.

Given my experience with Max, I feel like now would be a good time to address the mental health elephant in the room. While my goal for this book is to be as gender-neutral as possible, it would be misleading to not acknowledge that there is even more stigma surrounding men's mental health than mental health in general. To help us understand why this is and how to combat it, I reached out to Zac Seidler, a clinical psychologist who works with Movember, a men's health charity. You might be familiar with Movember's work if your coworker ever randomly showed up to work with a mustache in November. But since its origin, Movember has grown from focusing on promoting awareness of prostate cancer to an international organization that tackles all aspects of men's health. A large part of that is men's mental health and suicide prevention. (I also want to note that while Zac talks about men as a whole, all men are different and gender is fluid. Since we'll be talking generally, a lot of what follows might ring false to your experience or the experiences of those closest to you. Please assume that when we say "men" moving forward, what we mean is "most" or "some.")

One of the first things I asked Zac was why men are less likely to seek help, which can be super frustrating for their partners. The answer was complicated. For starters, many men feel pressure to appear a certain way. While they may not even believe in "masculine norms," which can include "self-reliance, stoicism, and strength," men "still feel the pressure to live up to them." Zac also points out that while stigma surrounding mental health in general is on the decline, "self-stigma exists, which is to say, 'I will help out my friend if he is struggling, but the second I have any symptoms, I can't do anything about them.' What mental health issues or difficulties often trigger in guys are these feelings of dependence, weakness, and vulnerability, and those very feelings are in direct contradiction with traditional masculinity. So you get to the point where they start to feel that they're a burden, and then you add in the shame and guilt of feeling inadequate, feeling like they can't look after themselves, and you end up with this silent crisis."

Zac says that another major reason men have more trouble not only seeking help but being successfully treated is because "the way they express their depression or anxiety is through externalizing symptoms—anger, irritability, violence, substance use. All of the shit that is 'boys being boys' is often a cry for help. If we overlook that, you get guys coming in and being treated for anger management, which doesn't do anything. And then when they do seek help and they end up with a psychologist in the right situation, they often drop out because they don't get what they need. Men are coming to see us and we are telling them, 'You need to be emotionally communicative, you need to cry, you need to do all these things that we understand as distress' and they're going, 'I don't want to do that. I don't know how to do that.' And we go, 'We'll teach you.' That's not how things should work. It should be, 'What do you want, what are your strengths, what are your capabilities, and how can I adapt to that accordingly?'"

Obviously what Zac is talking about is a systemic issue that won't be solved any time soon and requires a new interpretation of therapy, not just from the client's point of view but also from mental health professionals. But, even if the system can't change overnight, we can take what he's saying and apply it to ourselves and our relationships. The most helpful takeaway here is that anxiety and depression might not present in the same way for men as we've come to expect. If you or your partner are extremely irritable and prone to anger all the time, that's just as much of a clue into one's mental state as other more "typical" signs, like sleeping too much or having panic attacks. It's also helpful to recognize that it can be even harder for men to enter treatment in the first place, so providing extra encouragement and doing thorough research to find the right therapist for him might be necessary.

All that said, this doesn't mean men get a pass when it comes to addressing their mental health. When you're encouraging a man to get help, Zac says, "You want them to feel empowered and see the potential for change. That's always how I sell it: 'You don't need to continue living like this. That doesn't sound fun.' They believe that they deserve to suffer, and so they do that and, sadly, they take down everyone in their sphere as well. My first step is trying to get them to realize it doesn't need to be this way." Even if they were brought up thinking masculinity is synonymous with silently suffering, they can choose to put in the work and break that cycle.

Next I talked to Zac about how men can overcome their (understandable) fear of sharing their mental health history with a new partner. He said, "I make it very clear that if they're ashamed of it, then they're going to be ashamed of themselves and they are going to struggle to connect because they are not putting their whole selves into the relationship." He then added another reason why it's so critical to be vulnerable: "What do you think the benefit is in suggesting you are Superman? Where do you get the idea that you telling them you are unbreakable is going to be of any use to you in the long term?" This might be one of those quotes you want to write down in your notebook, because it applies to all of us. None of us are Superman, and that's a good thing. Superman is the most boring superhero because he doesn't have any flaws other than an intense allergic reaction to a certain type of rock. We are all complex, and in order to be complex, we have ups and downs mixed together. Whenever I meet someone who appears "perfect" or "untouchable," I might admire them, but they're not someone I want to wake up next to. Plus, if I did wake up next to them every day, eventually they would have morning breath and my perception of them would be shattered. It's much better for everyone to try to portray their true self from the beginning.

Zac also thinks it's important to destroy the harmful expectation that romantic partners have to "prop up and save so many men." The responsibility of men's stability and happiness shouldn't fall on their partners. Instead, men need to finally step up to the plate: "The idea that they are just little boys who have no idea about what to do is bullshit. There is endless potential. There are heaps of strength and ability that people overlook when it comes to men looking after themselves and men looking after other men as well." So if your partner is resistant to getting professional help and instead relies on you or someone else in his life to fill in the role of a therapist, you're allowed to call bullshit. This is an unhealthy pattern Zac has seen more than once. "I have plenty of clients and friends who are serial monogamists because being on their own and thinking through their life is just so overwhelming that they use a relationship as a crutch. You get those stereotypes around the partner, the wife, or girlfriend being a mother figure to them and playing that role of hoisting up their self-esteem, which is a very dangerous place to be. And that's why you end up with lots of pretty poor relationships continuing," says Zac.

If this scenario feels familiar to you because you're actively living it, don't despair. While there needs to be a lot of systemic change in order to make therapy more effective and welcoming for men, you're still allowed to put your foot down. But instead of focusing on their behavior, Zac suggests focusing on your experience: "You turn it around to start to get them to reflect on what the impact of their behavior is on you, the partner." This might help them better understand that they aren't the only casualty of their symptoms. Zac also suggests couples therapy as a segue into dealing with their individual issues. This is especially effective if your partner has never been in therapy before and is too afraid or hesitant to go alone.

A little bit of psychoeducation might also be beneficial because not everyone is aware that mental health issues often cause physical issues. Zac says, "If they're having sleep issues or they have somatic symptoms and headaches all the time and chronic pain, those are telltale signs that something is going on underneath. Because if you bottle something up endlessly, it comes out in physical symptoms." Ultimately, though, you can provide information, you can provide support, and you can even provide a therapist's phone number, but you can't make someone change. As Zac puts it, "If you're extremely unhappy and you love this person and they're not willing to change, that is an indictment on their personality, sadly, and if they're not willing to do the hard yards for you, let alone for themselves, then it's probably time to call it."

But what do you do if you aren't ready to walk away just yet? What if you want to make sure you've tried everything before breaking ties? One fancy word comes to mind in this scenario, and it's spelled u-l-t-i-m-a-t-u-m. This tactic has a negative connotation, but sometimes it feels like your only option. When I asked Annette about whether it's healthy to issue one to a partner who is refusing to get help, she said, "You shouldn't give an ultimatum unless you really mean it and plan to follow through with it. 'Ultimatum' almost sounds like a strategic ploy. I don't think of it as strategic. I think of it as an honest communication. You might say, 'I don't see myself staying in this if you don't get help,' and not 'If you don't get help, I'm going to leave.'"

Ultimatums, as we often think of them, are completely contingent on *the other person's behavior* and can therefore make that person feel defensive and attacked. "Speaking your truth," as I like to call it, is simply alerting someone to a probable outcome if nothing changes; aka: "I don't want my life to continue in this way, so I will take whatever actions are necessary for that not to be the case." Instead of focusing on how to influence someone else's behavior, reframe the situation as you taking control over your own behavior. You don't want to be with someone who won't help themselves, so you are choosing to leave. That's not manipulation; that's self-preservation.

I think the biggest takeaway from this chapter is that, in addition to checking in with yourself along the way, you need to pay attention to what your partner is telling you both directly and indirectly. If it's clear the relationship is going to be an uphill battle from the start, listen to your gut and know it's probably not worth investing your time and energy. This is especially true when you already struggle with your mental health. Entering and engaging in an unhealthy romantic relationship is a surefire way to throw your stability off balance. While love is wonderful, it's not worth being miserable 60 percent of the time (and let's be honest, it'll probably be more like 80 percent if you're prone to rumination). So take the extra time and effort to analyze yourself and your partner before committing to anything serious. Are you both in the right headspace to date? Are you equally supportive of each other? Are your experiences and point of view validated and accepted? Are theirs? Are you both doing the individual work necessary to be your best selves? And, if all those things were true at the beginning of the relationship, are they still true now, however many months or years later?

As a final reminder, healthy relationships aren't devoid of conflict. Instead, they are often defined by how conflict is handled. Annette explains, "You shouldn't be having the same fight over and over again in the same way. You might have it a few times, but hopefully there is some learning occurring along with the arguments, some closeness that's developing, so you know more about each other. You know more about what sets someone off and what would work better to resolve conflicts. So you can have the fights less often, they get less intense, and you recover from them more quickly and with less strain."

There are also going to be different stages and adjustment periods throughout your partnership. Moving in together might bring some idiosyncrasies to light that weren't clear before. (For example, when I lived with my ex, I asked him to strip naked and immediately shower after being on an airplane due to my contamination OCD. And the fact that airplanes are disgusting!) Everyone has their quirks, and as Annette puts it, "Oftentimes people think their 'quirk' is reasonable or right or makes the most sense or is morally superior. And that can be really maddening. We should all be aware that we are bringing idiosyncrasies to the table and you have to check some of them." These compromises she's talking about come in all shapes and forms. Sometimes it means cleaning your hair off the shower wall because it grosses your partner out and sometimes it means getting the professional help you need even when you don't want to. Hopefully your partner makes it all worth it and you wind up in an even better place than where you started. That's a surefire sign of a healthy relationship.

We've arrived at the end of another chapter! What a journey! Before we turn the page both literally and figuratively, it's time for our bullet-point recap! Go team!

- Sometimes you are simply not in the right place to date. And that's okay!

- Before diving into dating, assess how you are doing mentally by looking at your current functionality in all areas of your life.

- The dynamics you establish at the beginning of the relationship will most likely continue throughout the relationship.

- Try to only date people who are supportive and open-minded when it comes to therapy and psychiatry.

- Unhealthy relationships will take a huge toll on your mental health. So, you know, try to avoid them.

- If your partner needs help but refuses to get it, you need to tell them that you will not be able to stay in the relationship if nothing changes.

- You and your partner are a team! If you look at them as your adversary, you're only attacking yourself.

I can't believe I told you that story about the time I got diarrhea! I am clearly VERY invested in this. Hope you are, too!

CHAPTER FOUR

HOW DO I TALK ABOUT MENTAL HEALTH WITH MY PARTNER?

TRIGGER WARNING: Mentions of self-harm

want to start this chapter off with a simple but important acknowledgment: It is not an easy thing to share your mental health history with your (potential) partner. I actually think "terrifying" and "confusing" are good descriptors for this vulnerable process. There are so many variables at play and very little mainstream guidance. *When* should you tell them? *How* should you tell them? Should you tell them everything all at once or spread it out over days? Weeks? Months? The answers are unclear, even to me, so I'm turning to two of our favorite therapists to help us navigate this rocky terrain. We'll also hear from two couples who've successfully communicated their mental health struggles to each other. Despite their different backgrounds, everyone I spoke to agreed that disclosing your mental health history is not just a conversation worth having, it's a conversation that needs to happen if you want to have a full-blown, healthy relationship.

Sheva, the licensed marriage and family therapist we met in chapter two, says that when it comes to having these conversations, it's important to honor and acknowledge stigma's inevitable presence: "It's not completely wild to assume that your partner might have thoughts and feelings about what you're going through. There is that whole bit of cultural evolution we haven't quite hit yet where it's okay to struggle with something mentally, because our brain is just another part of our body." In other words, it's reasonable to have extreme hesitation when it comes to talking about all of this. It doesn't make you weak or self-hating. It makes you a cognizant member of our current misinformed reality.

While *we* might be completely aware of and familiar with the mental health community, not everyone is coming to the table with that same knowledge and experience. Sheva adds, "The statistics say that one in five people will be diagnosed with a mental health disorder in their lifetime, and that doesn't include the probably hundreds of thousands of people who don't realize or report. There is nothing to be ashamed of. But it's personal information, it's sensitive information, and so when you decide to disclose, it's very much a personal choice [based on] the level of safety and comfort you feel in that relationship." Some might feel comfortable and ready after, say, five dates, or maybe even two. For others, it might take more time, and that's okay and understandable. It's better to judge the "right" moment by the stage of the relationship rather than any fixed period of time.

Annette, the couple's therapist from chapter three, agrees: "Relationships unfold in different ways. There is no one-size-fits-all rule." But she acknowledges that if you are getting to the stage where "you're starting to open up about your life in general, your family, things in your past, and you leave that out, it is a false narrative of your life." We all know there are different levels of "getting to know each other" conversations. "What are your hobbies?" is different from "When did you lose your virginity?," which is different from "My mom is an alcoholic." If you're still in the "here's a funny-but-tame story from work" part of courtship, you're not obligated to divulge your entire mental health history while bowling or whatever kids do for fun these days.

As your discussions turn more intimate, however, Annette says, "That's a point where you might open up and say, 'I've had anxiety issues. I've gotten help with them over the years.' Does that mean right then you would take out your notebook and say, 'I want to tell you about every anxiety attack'? No." Instead, you disclose a little and see how the other person responds. "If you say, 'I had a terrible relationship with my mother,' and she or he says, 'Cool. What are we eating for dinner?' that would be a clue to you that this isn't someone who is that emotionally interested." So even though you're the one who is sharing, how your potential partner responds is deeply revealing of their character and how much they value your potential relationship. As Annette puts it, "Interest is a huge part. How much do they want to know you deeply? How caring, supportive, interested, and nurturing is this person you're getting to know? How comforting are they? If they don't want to know you deeply and you have significant mental health issues, they're probably not a good fit."

Sheva adds (quite beautifully, I think), "If someone gets scared off because you shared a part of yourself, that's important data about their capacity to hold your complexity." This is yet another reminder that relationships are a two-way street. Just as they might rebuff you for your history, you have every right to rebuff them for how they handle your history.

When I was younger, I had a "take me or leave me" mentality. I also had a tendency to word-vomit and put it all out there immediately. While I proudly believed this was coming from a place of self-acceptance, Sheva suggested there might have been another motivator. She says that if you tend to reveal everything right away, "it could be coming from your anxiety: 'I'm so afraid that you're going to reject me that I'm just going to put everything out on the table now and wish us luck.'" In order to combat compulsive sharing, Sheva suggests paying attention to your delivery style: "What energy is behind your disclosure? Is it something like, 'This is uncomfortable for me so I'm just going to pour everything out without any regard for how I'm presenting it'? If that's the case, your partner might react not to the *facts* of your disclosure but to your *anxiety* surrounding the disclosure." It makes sense that your partner might feel uncomfortable if you're radiating discomfort. So while it's unlikely you'll be cool as a cucumber during such an intimate conversation, try your best to speak as clearly and calmly as possible. This will help create a safe space for both of you.

You also don't have to disclose everything all at once. What parts are most relevant to who you are now? While my mental illness used to take up so much of my time and energy, I'm lucky to announce that this is no longer the case. I'm not thinking about it as much, so I'm not talking about it as much. In my last relationship, I shared the gist of everything pretty early on, but I didn't feel as compelled to get into the nitty-gritty things that, in some cases, had happened decades prior. It wasn't until my ex was reading a draft of this book that he even learned I cut myself in college. I wasn't purposefully keeping this from him. It just honestly never came up or felt relevant to who I am today.

All of this said, I know that some people might find it debilitatingly difficult to even *initiate* these important conversations. Not everyone is as comfortable talking about all this stuff as me, a person who gets paid to write about mental health. If you're the opposite of me and dread talking about your mental health, Sheva says you should "explore what your anxieties around disclosure might be." Try to process them: *What am I afraid of? Am I internalizing the stigma that is in our society?* It wouldn't be [unusual] to feel this by any means. It's real. If you're internalizing that same stigma—*I am flawed because I have a mental health condition*—then that could be a block for you in terms of being comfortable enough to disclose." If you're already in therapy, this is definitely something worth discussing with your therapist. If you're not in therapy, Sheva says it might be beneficial to role-play the conversation with a trusted confidant: "Practice how you want to say this to somebody. Choosing the right setting is important, too. Even choosing a time when both you and your partner are chilling out on a Sunday afternoon. A balanced time and place. It's okay to feel nervous about it."

What's important to remember, according to Annette (and me), is, "Hopefully by the time you're really liking someone, you're liking them because they're good to you, they're a good person, they're kind." So give them the benefit of the doubt and trust that they will receive your truth with an open heart and inquisitive mind.

There are obvious benefits to sharing your mental health history with a new partner. It creates intimacy and transparency, but it also clues your partner in to how your brain operates. That said, it can often feel overwhelming, if not downright impossible, to explain anxiety, OCD, and/or depression to someone who has never experienced it. That's why Sheva says it's important to have realistic expectations: "Your partner doesn't have to completely understand you in order to be there for you. It's really hard to understand certain mental health disorders if you've never experienced that kind of mental stickiness. Your partner doesn't have to 100 percent get it in order to be 100 percent supportive and in order to see that you're going through something and be there for you through that struggle." And let's be honest, it's impossible to fully understand how anyone else's brain operates, even if they're neurotypical. What's more important than complete comprehension is empathy and validation—"I might not feel this way or see the world this way, but I acknowledge and respect that you do."

Of course, it is helpful for your partner to have as much insight as possible. You can do your best to explain how your mental illness interferes with your life, what coping mechanisms are helpful, and how you would prefer your partner to respond when you're not doing well or in crisis. You can also use descriptive language to try to better portray what you've experienced. Annette gives an example of how you might explain anxiety: "When I try out for a play, the kid next to me is like, 'I hope I sing well and do a good job,' and I'm thinking, *There is a tiger offstage that is about to come and attack me and I might not be alive at the end of this.*"

Pulling from specific experiences instead of speaking generally might further clarify things. I've often described to others how sometimes I'll be walking around totally fine, only to suddenly feel as though I've become contaminated, and my mind won't relax until I can take a shower. There has been no physical change to the cleanliness of my body. It is a purely mental shift. I'm sure this is a strange and probably foreign experience for some people to hear about, but it's also a clear example of my personal experience with contamination OCD. Plus, it's completely different from the symptoms of other subsets of OCD, and that clarification matters because people might not realize that OCD can manifest in various ways, depending on the person. Sheva adds, "The more that person educates themselves on the neurobiology of mental illness, the more distance they're going to be able to have from the condition." In other words, it will help your partner take things less personally when they understand what's happening inside that confounding brain of yours because they'll realize it has little to nothing to do with them. It also helps them distinguish your symptoms from your personality.

Luckily—or unluckily, depending how you look at it—many people live with these disorders, so your partner doesn't need to rely solely on your personal narrative to gain understanding. They can look to other resources such as books and credible websites for more information on your disorder(s). Another possibility, according to Sheva, is to invite your partner to a therapy session. She says, "It can definitely be helpful. One thing I like to do when I have those kinds of sessions is offer the partner some alone time [with me] because they might want to ask questions that might be painful for the sufferer to hear, but questions that nonetheless need to be answered and are answered with the gentleness of the therapeutic relationship. Difficult questions like, 'Is this genetic? Will my children have this? What do I do when they have an episode or a spike and they really tear me down?' These can be hurtful things for the sufferer to hear, but the partner needs time to process that." Obviously you don't want your third date to be in your therapist's office, but I think it's a great option once you've decided to enter into a committed relationship.

Sheva touches on another important point: Your partner might have some serious questions and concerns after learning about your history. They might even wonder if they are up for the task of dating someone with anxiety, OCD, and/or depression. And do you know what? That's fine! Sheva says it's important to normalize this reaction and not villainize it. What matters most is how they then deal with this fear and/or worry. According to Annette, the first step is for them to understand where that worry is coming from. "What are they worried about? Not being supportive enough? That the problem will dictate their lives? They might need some help to understand the nature of it. If the person is worried, the conversation should be a forthcoming one where their partner is really honest and tells them what's involved," she says. And just because someone is worried doesn't mean they're going to jump ship. Annette says, "What's going to get them over the hump of tackling that worry is genuinely being invested in you." And I think this is true. The more connected you are to someone, the more willing you are to fight for the relationship, even if that fight is an internal one.

Sheva adds that it's also important for your partner to have "their own support system that is separate from the relationship. It doesn't mean they have to go to therapy. It does mean they get to have a space where they can vent and express themselves, where they don't have to package their words in any particular way. We all need that." While you might initially see your partner venting about your disorder(s) as a betrayal, your partner needs the freedom to discuss it with an impartial party in order to protect and save the relationship. This way, the person suffering isn't burdened with their partner's frustration, and the partner still has an outlet to feel their feelings and process the situation. Bottling things up and/or relying solely on each other is the antithesis of a healthy relationship. If you're in a bad place and it's clearly taking a toll on your relationship, encourage your partner to seek additional support for themselves. Give them that permission to care for themselves without feeling guilty. Hopefully they've been doing the same for you!

There's one more thing for your partner to consider when contemplating their relationship with you: Nothing in life is foolproof.

Romantic relationships involve risk, regardless of whether or not someone is dealing with mental health issues. As Sheva puts it, "All relationships are unknown. You could date someone who has a clean bill of health and the next day they could have a paralysis attack. There are absolutely no guarantees when it comes to what your future may hold with a person. Risk is a part of it." And, she says, depending on how you look at it, starting a relationship with someone who has been to the dark side and returned might actually be a good thing: "You're with somebody who knows how to go through shit. And there's a lot of value in that." So much value, in fact, I think we should all take an applause break to honor ourselves and our struggles.

(Hold for applause break.)

Welcome back! Way to clap for yourself! That takes a lot of moxie! Especially if you're reading this in public!

———

Okay, we've officially tackled how to approach initial conversations about your mental health history! Wahoo! But as many of you may know, relationships are basically never-ending conversations with your partner, and mental health is bound to come up again (and again). It's one thing to tell someone about something that's already happened. It's trickier to discuss something while it's actively happening. One thing I've struggled with in the past is feeling like I need to prepare my partner for potential declines in my mental health. Like, "Sure, the person you see before you right now is chill and capable, but you haven't seen me at my worst. Are you prepared for that?! ARE YOU?!" I asked Annette if it's a good idea to warn your partner that you might not always be in a good place. She says, "I think the question is to what end. Is it a good idea if you love someone and you're worried about them and you're also worried about yourself—whether they'll be able to handle what could happen? Yes, it's a good idea. I have an example of somebody who had a ton of anxiety and shared her whole history with someone she really loved. She seemed to be in such a good place, he couldn't believe it or quite understand. And he responded, 'Listen, you're telling me these things, but they make no sense to me. That is not the person I see in front of me.' And he asked, 'Is it okay if I bring this up with your family? Because I want to understand this better. I want to make sure that I get it and I can do a good job of taking care of you.' And she said, 'Yes, please.' And he did! But for a while he continued to say, 'I don't really get it. I believe you all. But I don't really get it.'"

That's the problem with any sort of warning. You can try to understand things on an intellectual level, but can you ever fully comprehend something before you experience it for yourself? My gut is leaning toward maybe/no. Despite the flawed outcome, the desire to warn makes sense. Even when I was doing well, I used to live in fear of the dark days returning. Memories of my anxiety and depression would haunt me. Why wouldn't you want to prepare those closest to you for what feels like the inevitable? Everyone on *Game of Thrones* kept shouting "WINTER IS COMING" for a reason. But the thing we sometimes forget is that climates (and people) have a tendency to change. And while you might still have *worse* days, the *absolute worst* may well be behind you. Annette says, "Sometimes, the more we understand about ourselves, the more our treatments are solid treatments, the more our medication is solid, each cycle isn't necessarily like the one before. One could say,

'I want you to know it could happen again, but I am hopeful that I'm in a better place to deal with what comes up.'" And if you don't feel like you'd be able to deal with it, that might be one of those pesky signs that you're not ready to dive into a serious relationship.

If you *do* feel like you're in a good place overall but are suddenly having a rough time—for whatever reason—I'd argue that you have a responsibility to clue your partner in (and vice versa). This doesn't (and shouldn't) mean you tell them every distressful thought that is running through your head. But it's helpful to give them a simple heads-up. For example, "I'm feeling super anxious lately. I think I'm going to talk to my psychiatrist about it." Or, "I'm worried my depression might be back so I'm going to start waking up early to do yoga." This type of disclosure accomplishes two crucial things: (1) It acknowledges the change in your behavior and alleviates any fear they might have that they are the cause, and (2) it tells them that you have plans to address the situation. We all know there aren't quick fixes when it comes to mental health, but it's a lot easier to have patience when there is a plan in place versus waiting for things to magically change.

When you live with anxiety and/or OCD, one thing you have to be cautious of during a flare-up is oversharing. Yes, you should fill your partner in on the basics, but you don't need to divulge the specifics. We discussed this in chapter two, but to reiterate, Sheva says, "I always talk with clients about the difference between *process* and *content* and relaying that information in your relationships. You want to think about the process, which relays to them 'I'm anxious,' 'I'm triggered,' 'I feel dysregulated,' 'I feel overwhelmed,' 'I feel depressed.' That's the process of what's going on. That's important to express because that relieves the other person of their struggle with the unknown: *What is she feeling? Is it me? Is it something*

I said? You're tuning the other person in to your experience. But what I don't recommend people divulge, especially when it comes to anxiety disorders, is content." For example, "I'm worried I don't miss you enough when you leave and this means I could be in the wrong relationship." It's best to keep that little gem to yourself after you correctly label it an anxiety thought and move on with your life.

Sometimes, though, the content of your worry is directly related to what's going on and this makes it harder to keep it to yourself without feeling like you're secretly withholding from your loving partner. Let's say you live with social anxiety and you have to attend your partner's office party. Should you tell them you're internally freaking out at the thought of munching on crudités with their boss? Yes, but only to an extent. And only once you know your own motivation for disclosing those fears. Sheva explains, "It's very important to be able to identify: *When am I acting compulsively versus when am I seeking support?* I think if that distinction can be identified, you're able to frame your disclosure more productively." If you simply share that you're excited to support your partner at their work event but you're feeling socially anxious about meeting a bunch of new people, that's a helpful thing for your partner to know. This way they'll make sure to not leave you alone until you're settled and may be open to leaving early. What's not helpful, according to Sheva, is, "sitting in the car on the way there going, 'What if this person doesn't like me? What if everyone thinks I'm stupid and boring?' And your partner is just feeding into that reassurance. That's no longer helpful."

The need for reassurance will probably play a large part in your relationship if you live with OCD and/or anxiety. (Those in the throes of depression are more likely to believe their thoughts that nothing matters and life is meaningless.) Seeking continuous reassurance is one of the hardest habits I've had to break. If we're being completely honest, I haven't quite nailed the landing. But I *have* come up with a helpful rule of thumb. I still let myself ask for reassurance about certain things, but I only let myself ask once (per day).

It might not be immediately apparent that you're seeking reassurance if you don't stop to think about it. So here are some examples of what I'm tempted to seek reassurance about, in case they ring any bells:

- Is my dog happy?

- Did my workout count? (Basically, did I work hard enough/ burn enough calories?)

- Does my dog know I love her?

- Did I do enough work today?

- Was I rude to that person by accident?

- Am I a good dog mom?

As you can see, most of my need for reassurance revolves around my rescue dog, Sugar, who is honestly pretty fucking chill and probably fine. For other people, it might revolve more around the relationship: *Do you still love me? Will you always love me? Why do you love me?* While it feels wonderful in the moment to hear your partner reply, "Yes, of course, so many reasons," they will never be able to fully satisfy your anxiety if you're asking compulsively. Plus, it's eventually going to get annoying for them. When you ask someone the same question over and over again, it implies that you don't believe their answer. This is why I suggest implementing the One Ask Rule for *both* parties, because your partner might also have a habit of asking for reassurance about completely different things. For example, while I tend to fixate on Sugar's emotional well-being, my most recent ex constantly questioned whether he was making enough upsales at work. There were only so many different ways for me to say "Yes, you are." So even though the content of each partner's worries might vary, the process of trying to relinquish those worries is the same and isn't fun or productive for anyone. To put it simply, no amount of external validation is going to be enough to scratch that reassurance itch. That's why it's so important to figure out how to self-soothe.

That said, there *are* times when we need extra support from our partners (or vice versa). This is a normal part of any relationship, but it's important to make sure a caretaker/patient dynamic doesn't take over. While some actively seek out the caretaker role, I'm going to assume most of you are striving for equal partnerships. So how do you maintain this balance when one person is struggling? Annette says, "Part of being equals is the person who is struggling having some semblance in their mind that someone else is there. You might be really anxious, but you still might be able to remember that your partner needs some comfort or appreciation or reassurance." If you're the one going through it, make sure you're taking time outside your own brain to check in on how your partner is doing. Let them know that you recognize and appreciate what they're going through as well.

And if you're the partner who's noticed your person seems to be struggling more than normal, Annette says that sharing your concerns can "be really loving and helpful. 'I'm worried that you're feeling down because you don't seem yourself. I'm worried that your anxiety is getting the best of you and small things are feeling so hard.' Saying to someone, 'You're just boring, depressed, and annoying'? No. That's not good. But sharing that you're concerned about them should be a good thing."

This is another example of being cognizant of not just *what* you're communicating, but *how* you're communicating it. The words you choose and the way you frame the situation are important. Sheva warns that sometimes the person who isn't doing well might initially get annoyed and defensive, but "if it's affecting the partnership, if the anxiety is affecting the connection, then I do think it's appropriate for the other person to gently and kindly point that out. I don't think it's helpful for them to say, 'This is your OCD.' But it is helpful to reflect back: 'Could this be anxiety talking, and if so, how can I best support you?'" The use of the word "support" is crucial. Make sure it's clear you're not coming from a place of judgment or irritation and that being supportive is your number one goal. Partners are *meant* to help and support each other. That's sort of the whole point of buddying up in the first place! (And also so no one gets left behind on a school field trip.)

Despite the best of intentions, broaching a sensitive topic can still be challenging. Here are some examples of what to say versus what not to say:

SCENARIO: Your partner has been stressed out about work, and as a result, their OCD symptoms are flaring up.

Helpful things you can say:

- Is there something I can do to help you so you don't have to worry about anything other than meeting your deadline? Maybe I can take out the trash or bring you dinner?

- Work seems to be expecting a lot from you right now. Are you getting any time to unwind? Self-care is important!

- Is there anything that might help lower your stress while you push through all this? I know you mentioned meditation has helped in the past.

Unhelpful things to say:

- Why do you keep cleaning the apartment when you have work to do?

- You need to call your therapist. You're acting crazy.

- Your stress is stressing me out.

SCENARIO: Your partner appears to be struggling with a depressive episode and doesn't want to do anything other than watch TV when they get home.

Helpful things you can say:

- Do you think you might be depressed? Is this what it felt like last time?

- I'm so sorry you're feeling down and unmotivated. That must be so frustrating.

- What are some things that helped the last time you felt this way?

Unhelpful things to say:

- You need to fix this ASAP.

- Ugh. You're being super boring.

- Let's just go do something! Come on! Let's go! *whistle as if they are a dog* (Pro tip: Never whistle at your partner as if they are a dog. Also, avoid clapping your hands on your thighs while speaking in a baby voice unless you get verbal consent ahead of time.)

While I can shout advice until I'm blue in the face—or my fingers hurt from impassioned typing—sometimes real-world examples provide more clarity. So let's get to know some real-world couples!

Gloria and Sam have been dating for almost three years and don't live together. Taylor and Rebecca have been married for seven years and together for twelve. Since Gloria and Taylor have both been vocal about their mental health struggles (depression and OCD, respectively) on social media, I figured they would be open to talking about how they've communicated with their partners about their mental health. And I was right! (Sidenote: There is so much power in sharing our stories with each other. You never know who you might be helping simply by letting others know they are not alone in their struggles. Plus, we're all about to learn a whole lot!)

Gloria's depression didn't become a real hindrance in her life until her mid-twenties. She realized, "I needed to be active in trying to get through this depression and the situation. So that's when I started going to therapy and started looking at the tools that are available through research and talking to a therapist. Probably for the last five or six years, it's been a journey of finding what works and doing really well, and then needing to find new things."

During this time, she crossed paths with Sam at work, but things didn't become romantic until about six months after Gloria went through a breakup with a different guy and started medication. "I finally started seeing a psychiatrist, and antidepressants were super helpful. I'm sure it's not a coincidence that I decided to pursue someone when I felt like I was in a much better place. I definitely felt more even-keeled than I'd felt in a long time," says Gloria. (As you can see, Gloria got herself into a good place mentally before successfully starting a new relationship. I love when my interview subjects prove my points for me!)

Despite the fact that she was doing better, Gloria wanted to tell Sam about her history and ongoing relationship with her mental health. When I asked Gloria if she recalled initiating this conversation, she replied, "I don't really remember." That's when Sam jumped in and said, "I remember it pretty specifically. Gloria broached it early on. I think we had only been seeing each other for a few weeks. And she brought it up with a lot of gravitas. Gloria basically sat me down and was like, 'There is something very important I need to tell you.' And I was like, 'Okay, what is it?' I was really worried. And Gloria said something like, 'I suffer from depression.' And I was like, 'Oh, okay. Yeah, that's fine.'"

Gloria's and Sam's differing recollections of this conversation are important for a couple reasons. For starters, Gloria was obviously extremely nervous going in, yet it ended up being such an easy exchange that she promptly forgot about it. This shows that anticipation anxiety can cause someone to overreact to things that haven't even happened yet. Meanwhile, this conversation left a lasting impression on Sam because it's powerful when someone opens up to you and trusts you with their most vulnerable information. It can also lead to unexpected outcomes. Sam says learning about Gloria's battle with depression was "in some ways reassuring" because, as it turns out, Sam has had his own mental health struggles. He thought they would be better able to understand each other due to these similar experiences. As Sheva said earlier, one in five people are diagnosed with mental disorders over their lifetime. So it's pretty likely that when you share your mental health struggles with a new partner, they will find something relatable about it, even if they've never been diagnosed with anything specific. (It's hard to be human and not have some significant ups and downs.)

When it came to Sam disclosing his own history, he didn't sit Gloria down and tell her everything all at once. While he went over the basics early on—issues with anxiety and depression, experience with therapists—one aspect of Sam's journey, self-harm, didn't come up until later. As someone with experience in self-harm, this makes total sense to me. While people instinctively get what it means to worry or feel down, it's harder to make the leap to understanding the desire to cause physical harm to yourself as a coping mechanism. Sam feels similarly: "It's definitely a much more difficult thing to talk about and, in my experience, much more alienating. It's harder for people to relate." Despite his reservations, when a character in a movie they were watching exhibited self-harming behaviors, Sam shared that he had similar episodes growing up. Seeing this behavior play out on-screen helped Gloria understand Sam better. When she questioned why the character in the film was hurting himself, Sam clarified that the character was upset about his actions so he was taking it out on himself physically. This explanation was revealing about Sam's own relationship with self-harm. And even though Sam no longer self-harms, understanding a partner's past experiences is never a bad thing.

This story is another reminder that you don't need to share your entire history in one sitting. You will (hopefully) learn more and more about each other over time, and an important part of that learning process will include figuring out how to react when you or your partner are struggling. It's taken some time for Gloria and Sam to grasp how to best interact with each other, because they have completely different coping skills. As a result, they've had to go against their natural instincts and learn what works for the other person. Sam explains, "It's easy to find yourself being prescriptive to your partner about how they should go about handling their struggles with mental health. But the things that make me feel better when I'm feeling the blues are not necessarily the things that make Gloria feel better. That falls into the bucket of not coming with a lot of preconceived notions about someone's mental health issues. Gloria and I both have anxiety, but it manifests in completely different ways. When Gloria feels anxious, she tends to shut down and be less active. I go into hyperactive mode." This is why it's so important to listen to your partner about what does and doesn't work for them.

Of course, it's impossible to know how to help your partner if they don't explicitly tell you. Gloria recounted a time early on in their relationship when she was going to be out of town for a couple months for work. One night, right before she was set to leave, Sam announced that he needed to head home and go to bed. Gloria took this as a personal insult. Didn't he want to spend as much time as possible with her before she left? In reality, Sam has serious issues with insomnia and if he's not vigilant about when he goes to bed, it can completely ruin his sleep schedule. (Studies show that sleep and mental health are so entwined, they might as well get a room.) At the time, Gloria wasn't aware of Sam's sleep issues, which is why it hurt her in the moment. Now that she's aware, Gloria also prioritizes Sam's sleep and knows that doing so benefits both of them. "Sam's a happier person the next day when he gets sleep. So it's an investment in the future," she says. This is a great way to look at accommodating your partner. What's good for them is good for you because you are a team.

Another thing Gloria had to learn is that while she is vocal about her suffering, Sam is not. Gloria explains, "I sometimes wonder if I'm doing a good enough job checking in on Sam, because he holds things closer to the chest. Sometimes it's harder for me to pick up on when something's a little more severe. I have to remind myself to check in with Sam, see how he's doing." So while it might not have come naturally for Gloria to do these "check-ins," it's now a part of her routine, so their support for each other is not lopsided. She goes out of her way to make sure he doesn't automatically fall into the caretaker role without his own needs being met.

ISN'T LOVE AND PERSONAL GROWTH WONDERFUL?!

Speaking of love and personal growth, it's time to get to know Taylor and Rebecca. They also met at work and are honestly one of the cutest couples I know. That's why it was surprising to learn that they almost broke up a few years into their relationship. The main source of their problems was a common culprit: bad communication. I was pretty shocked when Rebecca said, "I actually didn't find out Taylor had OCD until years into our relationship. We didn't have any arguments or fights for probably the first three years of our relationship. Everything was pretty smooth sailing. But once we started getting closer and getting to that level of a relationship where you really need to be vulnerable with each other and have serious talks, I noticed that Taylor would just shut down." It turns out that Taylor's

OCD and anxiety were affecting her ability to open up to Rebecca. Which, believe it or not, was a total surprise to Taylor.

One of the major tenets of therapy is psychoeducation about disorders. We've already touched on this briefly, but it's undeniably helpful to understand how your disorder(s) can manifest. While Taylor first suspected she had OCD as a teen after reading about it in a magazine, she wasn't formally diagnosed until years later. Despite getting the diagnosis, Taylor wasn't receiving treatment, and as a result, was unaware of how much her OCD was hurting her relationship with Rebecca. It was their couple's therapist who finally recommended Taylor see a psychiatrist. This is when Taylor's psychoeducation finally began. "I wasn't able to communicate, and I had this therapist and this psychiatrist being like, 'No, actually your anxiety and your OCD are preventing you from doing these things.' And I was like, 'What?!' I had no idea. It was a relief on so many levels, being able to talk to Rebecca and really tell her how I'm feeling in a way I hadn't been able to before. It was also this knowledge that there's nothing wrong with me. I'm a functional person. Mental illness has been getting in the way. And then I immediately went on medication and started to see a change within a few months. It was unbelievable," says Taylor.

Taylor wasn't the only one who benefited from this shift. Rebecca saw her partner flourish right before her eyes: "It was honestly mind-blowing for me to watch Taylor change into this person who could just push past the anxiety and be her fullest self." It also allowed them to have much better communication. Taylor explains, "So many of our issues boiled down to an inability to communicate and an inability to relate to one another because our brains were so different and the mental illness stuff was so intrinsically tied to that."

Before treatment, Taylor would often shut down and Rebecca would feel confused and stonewalled. When she learned that Taylor was actually dealing with an anxiety spiral in those moments, Rebecca said, "It was almost a relief. It has nothing to do with me. It has to do with these triggers. So it gave me an understanding, which I didn't have before, of what it would be like to be somebody with anxiety." Rebecca became aware of how confrontations might be a trigger. They now agree that the secret sauce to making a relationship work is good communication. And they weren't able to accomplish that until Taylor got a better handle on her mental health.

Rebecca repeatedly emphasized throughout our conversation that it took a lot of work for them to get to such a great place, especially since their brains operate so differently. "Relationships are not easy in general, but then when you have to try to understand something that is so foreign to you, that takes so much extra effort and work and energy—you need to want to go through it. There's something really great on the other side, but it's certainly not an easy process," she says. It's also an ongoing process. Rebecca explains, "[Your partner] is changing all the time. So either you continue to communicate and work through when things change, or you don't." As Rebecca suggests, it's important to repeatedly talk to your partner about your mental health and your sense of self because your relationship to both those things is bound to change with time.

A perfect example of this happened during our interview! A few minutes in, Rebecca did a pronoun check with Taylor, who has somewhat recently come out as nonbinary. Taylor shared, "I've always thought I knew myself so well. I remember being like sixteen and thinking I was such a self-aware teen, and then just learning new things about myself all the time and being like, *Wow,*

I am not nearly as self-aware as I thought. Now I'm thirty-eight, and over the past twelve to eighteen months, I realized I was non-binary. It's fascinating. You think you know yourself, you think you get yourself, but there are always going to be new things." Taylor's absolutely right—there will forever be new things to learn about yourself *and* about your partner. Give yourself the freedom to grow and change. Just make sure you're filling your partner in along the way. (At the time of the interview, Taylor approved the use of "she." Taylor's pronouns are they/she.)

Nothing we've said about the importance of communication is groundbreaking or unexpected. My guess is that about seven out of every ten couples would say that the key to their relationship is "good communication." What's left out of that answer is how much work needs to be done for it to actually happen. If you're bumping up against communication issues in your relationship, don't assume it's doomed to fail. Instead, make the commitment with your partner to learn as much as possible about how the other operates—even when it's really freakin' hard. As Rebecca puts it, "I think there's a level of vulnerability and even pain that comes with committing to a relationship when one or both of you struggle with mental health issues, and you just have to recognize that it's not personal. You might have to work through some more kinks than other people have to, but it will bring you to a deeper place."

Are you crying? Because I'm definitely not crying! No way, not at all! I'm too busy turning the biggest takeaways from this chapter into snappy bullet points:

- When sharing your mental health history with your (potential) partner, make sure you're doing it from a place of calm and not compulsion.

- Being vulnerable is scary but ultimately necessary for a healthy relationship.

- *How* you talk about something is just as important as *what* you are talking about.

- Your partner needs to have their own support system outside of the relationship, where they can talk freely and openly about their own worries, struggles, and fears.

- Mental health symptoms can present in many different and unexpected ways—make sure you explain how yours manifest.

- Listen to what your partner tells you, and don't assume your coping skills will work for your partner.

- Ongoing communication is essential, since people and relationships grow and change.

- Don't assume happy couples haven't had to put in a lot of work, despite what they post on Instagram! (This is a personal reminder.)

Even though Gloria, Sam, Rebecca, and Taylor are not their real names, their love is very real and beautiful, and I think of it often when I need a little extra faith in humanity. Maybe now you will, too!

CHAPTER FIVE

WILL MEDICATION HELP OR HURT?

MEET THE EXPERTS:

- **Dr. Jennifer Yashari** is a board-certified psychiatrist in private practice in Los Angeles, California. She has been practicing psychiatry for eighteen years. She sees adult men and women for both psychotherapy and/or medication management, treating a variety of conditions including mood and anxiety disorders. She also specializes in reproductive psychiatry, helping women navigate some of the most challenging phases of their lives: pregnancy, the postpartum period, infertility, and menopause. She incorporates cognitive behavioral therapy, psychodynamic psychotherapy, and mindfulness-based stress reduction techniques into her practice. We'll be referring to her as Jennifer.

- Remember **Dr. Zac Seidler** from chapter three? He'll be joining us again here! We'll (still) be referring to him as Zac.

hen I got sick with OCD in 1994, I was four years old and prescribing antidepressants to children was pretty much unheard of. Prozac had only been available to the public since 1988. Most people probably didn't even realize kids could experience mental illness, let alone need to be medicated. Luckily, my parents were way ahead of the curve, and within a few weeks of displaying symptoms, I had seen a specialist and was taking liquid Prozac in my apple juice. Yum! I don't know if I would have survived my childhood without medication. If I had survived, I know it wouldn't have been much of a childhood. I'm thankful every day that my parents understood the gravity of my OCD and responded accordingly, treating it the way they would any physical ailment. As a result, I've always viewed mental illness the same way. Viewing your mental health as a component of your overall health—and not some deficiency in your personality—is crucial. Not only does it alleviate self-judgment, but it also forces you to address any issues head-on and accept that sometimes you need assistance outside of therapy. Oftentimes that additional assistance comes in the form of medication.

You might be thinking, *Allison, this isn't a book about mental health. This is a book about mental health and dating. Why are we talking about this?!* Great question; thanks so much for asking! The main conceit of this book is that in order to have a healthy relationship, you have to have a good handle on your mental health. For many people, that includes going on medication as needed. Unfortunately, there continues to be a lot of anxiety and fear surrounding meds, and there is also a considerable discussion to be had about side effects. The point of this chapter isn't "Everyone should be on medication in order to be happy and get married!" Instead, I'm simply going to offer some clarity about psychotropics (medications that affect the brain) with the help of psychiatrist Dr. Jennifer Yashari and share my own experiences when it comes to side effects that may or may not play a role in your romantic relationships. Sound good? Clap twice if yes. I promise I can hear you.

I started off my call with Jennifer with such a basic question that it took her by surprise: Why the hell do medications cause side effects in the first place?! She explained, "Usually the way medications are designed is they target different receptors. And they can't always target the receptors in your brain as selectively as we would like. Take, for example, the serotonergic class of medications, SSRIs [selective serotonin reuptake inhibitors]. They're designed to target the serotonergic receptors in your brain. But because our gastrointestinal (GI) tract is also lined with serotonergic receptors, they sometimes inadvertently target those as well. That's why this class of medication can result in GI upset or nausea or vomiting or diarrhea." So basically the medications are doing the best they can, but until they are more refined (through what I can only imagine is years and years of research), side effects are going to occur for many patients. SSRIs are the type of drug most often prescribed for OCD, anxiety, and depression. The most common side effects associated with them are GI upset, weight gain, and sexual side effects. The good news is the GI issues should clear up after the first few weeks. The other two . . . not so much.

Over the years, I've been on pretty much every SSRI or SNRI you've ever heard of. (SNRI stands for serotonin–norepinephrine reuptake inhibitor, in case you were wondering. The difference has to do with which neurotransmitters are being targeted in your brain.) I've also dealt with quite a few side effects—not to brag or anything. The common side effect I want to talk about first is weight gain. Fear of weight gain is probably one of the main reasons people avoid going on antidepressants. And I get it. We live in a society that fetishizes the thin and morally condemns anyone with a BMI over 24.9. The much-needed body positivity movement has gained some traction in recent years, but as a millennial, I grew up absorbing a clear narrative: Thin is good. Fat, anywhere on your body, is bad. (I could probably write another whole book about why this type of thinking is so detrimental, but I am contractually obligated to finish writing this one first.) So I understand *why* people don't want to gain weight in our society, even if gaining weight isn't actually bad or good. It is just a neutral thing that happens sometimes.

I wish I could say that when I gained over twenty pounds on Zoloft in 2017, I didn't care. But years of media messaging and family influence are hard to ignore. For most of my twenties, I was proudly not medicated. I had weaned myself off of Cymbalta the summer before my senior year of college and was committed to facing my issues on my own. This was a huge mistake. I finally went back on medication following my devastating breakup with Dylan in 2017. I was suicidal and desperate to feel better. So my therapist referred me to a wonderful psychiatrist who, years later, I asked to interview for this very book. Huge reveal: Jennifer is also my personal psychiatrist! And she's a great one, as you'll soon see.

It might sound strange that *I* was resistant to medication as an adult after how much it benefited me growing up. (I was medicated from ages four to twelve and seventeen to twenty-one.) The only explanation I have is that the stigma outweighed any logic. I thought I didn't need it anymore. I thought I was "strong enough" without it. And then I fell apart, and it became crystal clear that neither of those things were true. So I was prescribed a high dosage of Zoloft and started to feel like a person again. I was feeling so good that I barely noticed the weight gain. But let me tell you who did notice: the internet! And my parents, who are also victims of a lifetime of anti-fat conditioning. I went home to New York one weekend in 2018 to visit and my father handed me a Post-it with the numbers "125–135" written in his nearly illegible handwriting. After asking me to read it out loud for some reason, he informed me that

125–135 is the "healthy" weight range for my age and height and he feared I was over it. I got on a scale for the first time in months and saw he was right. I was in the 140s, which, according to the Post-it, was both unhealthy and objectively bad.

This was not the first time medication had drastically affected my weight. From ages eight to twelve, my family and I assumed I had a slow metabolism and would always be on the heavier side. But then I decided to go off Paxil because I was doing better, and my body changed seemingly overnight, causing us to realize that the extra weight was a side effect and not my natural body. So years later, my dad, with the best of intentions, didn't want a medication significantly changing my body again. He urged me to talk to my psychiatrist and switch meds. When this extremely uncomfortable conversation happened, I was in a relationship with someone who did not care about my weight. He never made me feel bad about my body and immediately supported me when I ran to him crying post-Post-it. This relationship made it a lot easier for me to not obsess over my weight gain or the uncomfortable conversation with my dad. I doubt the same would have been true if I was single or in the beginning stages of dating someone.

A big part of dating, if you're sexually active, is sharing your body with another person. And if you don't feel good about your body, it can be hard to get truly close to someone or even have the confidence to put yourself out there in the first place. For anyone who already deals with body insecurity, the thought of adding any extra pounds might be a deal breaker. I totally get that. But I think it's important to not take medication off the table solely because of that fear.

In order to reframe the way we think about all this, I want to start off by examining why some people gain weight on these medications. Jennifer explains that for some patients, it's a simple matter of getting their appetites back because their mood has improved: "There is often a broader emotional bandwidth that allows for more room to think about eating. Sometimes they're not as rigid as they were before, so they have the capacity to enjoy food more. Those are the easier weight gains to manage because if you know you're eating more, you can actively work on controlling that." Honestly, this kind of weight gain seems healthy to me. People need to eat! It's one of life's main pleasures *and* it can nourish your body. (Have you had any fresh fruit lately? That stuff is amazing.) The trickier part of this equation is when you're not eating more than before but you're still gaining weight. Jennifer says, "That's when we wonder if there is some sort of physiological or metabolic dysregulation happening from the medication." So what the heck do you do?

First of all, not everyone is going to gain weight on the same medications. While I gained weight on Zoloft, there are plenty of people who haven't (including members of my own family). So it's not as if agreeing to go on antidepressants is the same thing as signing up for an extra ten pounds. It's also perfectly okay to tell your psychiatrist from the get-go that you are worried about gaining weight. While it might feel weird to walk into a doctor's office and make demands, Jennifer says it's completely within your right: "The fact that you walked in the door—that's a big deal. That takes a lot of courage. And to be able to have a voice and a willingness to be honest about what you'll do or not do hopefully makes a psychiatrist's job easier." Like in every other part of life, you need to be your own advocate. If you try a medication and you can tell it's negatively affecting your metabolism, you can work with your psychiatrist to try something else. Jennifer says to remember that "the weight gain doesn't happen like you wake up a week later and you've gained ten pounds. Let's wait and see. And if one pound is a deal breaker, then okay, we tried it. But if it's the medication that's the right fit, it would be a shame to say no because you're worried about weight gain and then when you actually try it, it doesn't cause that for you. It is so individual and specific." My father always says, "If you don't ask, you don't get!" I'd like to add: If you don't try, you won't know! (Trademark to come.)

The truth is that a significant number of people *will* gain weight on these medications. If it happens to you, then you have to explore your personal priorities. The Post-it incident wasn't the first time my parents brought up my weight gain. I had already had a conversation with my mother about it a few months prior, which resulted in me politely asking her to shut up. For the first time in years, my brain wasn't operating with an extra level of neurosis weighing it down. Zoloft gave me a sense of freedom I had never experienced. While I had obviously been on medication before, this was the first time I was combining medication with healthy mental practices and stronger coping skills. Prior to the breakup, I had started implementing positive thinking. I had done enough work on my own and with my therapist that when I added the extra support of Zoloft, I was able to reach a level of stability that seemed impossible before. I remember walking around my apartment proclaiming, "This is what other people's brains are like! Incredible!"

So when my mom first brought up the idea of me switching medications, I was resistant. I didn't want to lose what I had so recently gained. But over time, as stability became my new normal instead of a mental vacation I feared would end too soon, I started to reassess. It did feel uncomfortable to look in the mirror and not recognize my newly round face. My own body felt foreign to me in a lot of ways. So I decided to talk to my psychiatrist about it and we agreed to wean me off Zoloft and start me on a combination of Trintellix and Wellbutrin. Trintellix is a newer drug known to have fewer side effects. (Full disclosure: It's also pretty pricey. Further proving the need for universal health care! But again, that argument could fill up its own book and I am busy writing this one!)

Despite having my psychiatrist on board, I felt conflicted about my decision to switch. Was I letting my vanity get in the way of my mental health? How could I, a self-proclaimed mental health advocate, make a decision based on weight gain while simultaneously urging people to prioritize their mental health above all else? Maybe because all-or-nothing thinking doesn't actually serve anyone. Instead of thinking of one option as inherently "good" and the other as inherently "bad," I could take care of my mental health *and* find a medication that worked better for my metabolism. Also, it's perfectly appropriate, according to Jennifer, to try to find a "side effect profile that works for you." There might be some trial and error along the way, but any good psychiatrist will be working right alongside you to figure out the best match. It's a process, not a one-stop shop. Plus, your relationship to medication is never fixed.

For a long time, staying on a medication that caused me to gain weight was right for me. I have no regrets about this and found it surprisingly easy to not hyper-fixate on my extra pounds, which I discovered can be a *positive* side effect of the right medication. Jennifer explains, "If someone is not on medication and he or she is obsessed with weight, it's probably due in large part to untreated symptoms. So when you manage the anxiety more effectively, it might feel a bit more tolerable to carry a few extra pounds. When there's a real obsession around body image, it's important to recognize that it may not always feel that way once the noisiness around it dies down." So while the idea of an extra five pounds might feel absolutely intolerable to you right now, your brain might cut you some much-needed slack once you're on the right meds. Pretty cool loophole, don't you think?

Before we move on to other side effects, let's talk body acceptance on or off medication. Like I mentioned earlier, a big difference between sexual relationships and all other relationships is the involvement of body parts. I grew up being extremely critical of my body. I chemically straightened my hair. I got a nose job. I fixated on my stomach pouch even when I was 110 pounds. And let me just say, it is *exhausting* to hate your body. Plus, all bodies are different! Your natural weight and my natural weight are different. How your body responds to certain foods versus how my body responds to those certain foods is different. To hold everyone—regardless of race, age, or body shape—to the same white-centric universal beauty standards is, to put it simply, a financial scam meant to bolster the beauty and weight-loss industries. It also has the additional ramification of keeping women, in particular, preoccupied with their bodies, and it takes up time and money that could be put to much better use.

Whether you want to believe it or not, beauty standards are a major tenet of the patriarchy. (It's no wonder they have such a negative impact on our collective mental health.) Every time we bash our own bodies, we are only hurting ourselves. We act as if getting a six-pack will guarantee us a lifetime of happiness. It won't. Trust me. I have been super thin *and* suicidal. You can't practice self-talk effectively while simultaneously shitting on your physical form. Plus, when you constantly talk about something, you are reinforcing that thought in your brain over and over again. Not talking about your body in a negative way helps you to not be so hyper-focused on your "flaws" because you're not letting yourself fixate on them in the same way. When I urge you to treat yourself with kindness, I mean every part of you. Chances are, in the absence of your own criticism, you'll end up feeling better about yourself. And while people have different predilections when it comes to appearances, pretty much everyone agrees that confidence is attractive. Imagine if we all collectively focused on gaining self-confidence instead of losing fat cells? That's an extreme makeover I can get behind! (TLC, at least think about it!)

Okay, my PSA is officially over! Back to side effects! And sex! Aka, sexual side effects! The next chapter offers a deep dive into my own complicated history with sex and anxiety, but it's important to address the medication component. According to Jennifer, sexual side effects often present as "either decreased libido or delayed orgasm [in] anywhere from one out of two patients to one out of three patients. And those don't typically subside. Those are only reversed when you decrease the dose or stop the medication." Let's be real. This is a BUMMER. But once again, not everyone experiences sexual side effects. Jennifer says some people actually see an increase in their libido "because they aren't as distracted or preoccupied or self-conscious or just in their heads as much. In those instances, SSRIs can actually be really helpful." I'm so happy for those people! But let's focus on pretty much everyone else. (And remember that "sex" isn't contained to penetration and applies to any sexual/intimate act, despite what we're taught in health class.)

Whenever I think about sexual side effects, a super problematic episode of *Sex and the City* pops into my head. Charlotte has met yet another "perfect man," only for him to be unable to have penetrative sex due to Prozac. Charlotte, horrified that a man can't perform in the way she was conditioned to expect, asks if he would consider going off the medication. His response? No way. Prozac has enhanced his life so much that the sexual side effects are worth it. Charlotte's response? She dumps him. Remember how I said the episode was (super) problematic? While this episode aired decades ago, what we see as we're growing up shapes our understanding of the world as adults. It's no wonder people are wary of medication when this is the type of media representation many of us have been exposed to surrounding sexual side effects. I, for one, would like to see some on-screen representation of someone who doesn't view their partner's sexual dysfunction as a personal failing and instead looks at the situation holistically. As Jennifer puts it, "Do you value your partner's emotional quality of life?" Or do you only care about their ability to orgasm?

If you are someone who experiences sexual side effects and they have caused a negative interaction with a partner, it's important to recognize that your partner made it all about themselves. And by doing so, they neglected to prioritize your overall happiness, which freaking sucks. That said, your partner might be coming from a place of ignorance. In that case, it's worth explaining your history and why you are prioritizing medication at this moment in your life. Notice how I say "this moment." Jennifer explains, "There are different priorities at different times. Sometimes when life is going better, there might be room to experiment with decreasing medication to see how that goes. Other times, when you're really struggling with anxiety and depression, sex may be much lower on the scale of priorities." Knowing what you need to prioritize and when comes from self-awareness. It's a decision to be made with your psychiatrist, not your sex buddy. It's also a decision that can change as you change.

Zac, the psychologist we met in chapter three, admits, "I often find that the vast majority of guys want to change their medication if they're getting sexual side effects, and that's because it ties into their sense of masculinity." Although these side effects are disparaging to the client initially, Zac sees it as a possible, and much-needed, teaching moment: "It's just a matter of [asking], 'How are we going to accept the situation for what it is?' and realizing that intimacy comes in all shapes and sizes. The idea that penetrative sex is all there can be is something that men struggle with regardless. So that needs to be dealt with as well." Much more on penetrative sex later (since I know that's why you all bought this book).

Another major fear when it comes to medication is the idea that psychotropics will cause you to "lose your personality." As someone in a creative field, I've often wondered if I could be both happy and funny. This type of thinking is detrimental, even though I understand where it comes from. Comedy is often described as tragedy plus time. So how can you possibly have comedy without tragedy? Might I suggest listening to a toddler babble for a few minutes? Or telling an excitable dog it's time to go on a walk? Comedy is around us all the time. Some of it comes from a place of pain, but a lot of it comes from the perspective of no longer being in pain and appreciating life. I already know what it feels like to want to die. I don't need to feel that again to be able to accurately write about humanity or make fart jokes.

That said, my sense of humor has actually changed in the last few years. I used to be the queen of self-deprecating jokes. Almost every story I told would end with a dramatic "Kill me!" I was the punch line of my own life and, while it garnered laughs, it also took a toll on my mental health. I couldn't truly respect myself and constantly roast my existence at the same time. So I made a conscious decision to change, and although I might have to think a bit harder at a party, I'm still getting tons of laughs, baby. One time, when we were little kids, my older sister put me in a doll's high chair and I got stuck—the fire department had to use the jaws of life to get me out. People love that story and I don't shit on myself when I tell it.

To be fair, people's personalities encompass a lot more than their sense of humor. Jennifer says she's often encountered clients who worry that medication might change their true self. You'll be relieved to know "it does not alter your personality. In fact, it does quite the opposite. I try to reframe it for patients by explaining that you can lose your personality when it's buried under layers of anxiety, obsession, or depression. Medication actually makes room for your personality to come up and out so that you can be more present and engaged. If you're so obsessive and distracted or preoccupied or self-conscious, you're not being yourself. If anything, [medication] allows you to be yourself more than ever before." This is exactly what happened to me. I've always suspected that deep down I was actually a pretty easygoing, happy person. I was just too weighed down by my symptoms to show that part of me. My most recent ex once casually said "she smiles all the time" when referring to me and it made my heart hurt in a good way. I don't know if anyone would have said the same when I was fifteen, twenty, or twenty-five. It has been such a pleasure to get to know the real me in the last few years. Turns out, I'm a good time!

Jennifer does point out that when on higher doses, some clients will experience cognitive dulling, or "brain fog." And occasionally "people say that they can't cry. And it is an uncomfortable feeling to not be able to discharge that emotion. We're always talking about what the 'right' amount of ability to cry is. Because when you're so depressed and overwhelmed, you're crying all the time. There is a cost benefit to not crying, so that is why you're working with your psychiatrist to have some feelings without too many feelings, to be able to emotionally react without being emotionally overreactive."

Note, too, that this is all coming from the point of view of those living with anxiety, OCD, and/or depression. Those who experience mania might feel differently about medication, "because you might lose that level of intensity . . . but you lose it because that level of intensity is also very self-destructive. That is the balance of medication," says Jennifer. As you can see, nothing about going on medication for your mental health is cut-and-dried. Side effects are a reality. The only way to make the right decision for you is to weigh the cost benefit of *not* going on medication if you need it.

Of course, medication isn't automatically the best option for everyone who has anxiety, OCD, and/or depression. Even within the mental health community, there is disagreement on the benefits of medication, since people often make just as much or more progress with CBT or other forms of therapy. There is also significant evidence that the improvements made while on medication don't last after the person stops taking them, unlike the more long-lasting benefits of certain therapeutic interventions. So when should you seriously consider seeing a psychiatrist about adding medication to your treatment plan? Jennifer says, "Ideally, if stable enough, you start with therapy. You start to consider meds when you are taking in the work in therapy but you're having trouble truly applying it. You intellectually recognize how you'd like to be thinking about things, but emotionally you're so overwhelmed that you're not able to access those healthier thoughts or tools. Or you can't actually tolerate the level of emotional discomfort that's really required to do the deeper work in therapy. Medication can allow for that. If you're getting stuck in therapy, the therapist is usually really good at saying, 'You know, I think it might be time to see what medication can do for you in conjunction.' It's often both that get you to where you want to be."

If you're not currently in therapy and don't have the insight of a professional to help you make that decision, Jennifer says, "It's really about recognizing when symptoms start to interfere with your social and occupational and emotional functioning. It's one thing to be having a hard time and struggling. It's another thing if you're having such a hard time that you're not sleeping or eating or you're starting to engage in increasingly unhealthy coping mechanisms. That's when we get more concerned. It's really about the degree to which your functioning is impaired." She clarified further with what I found to be an extremely enlightening perspective: "You don't have to get to a point where you're so impaired that you need medication. It's okay to not want to be white-knuckling through life. You get one life and one internal emotional quality of life, and you get to decide how hard you want to work at maintaining a healthy mental baseline." Do you have chills? Because when she first said this, I sure did.

It's often hard to explain what it feels like to battle mental illness day-to-day when you're also able to meet all of your obligations. "White-knuckling through life" is one of the best descriptions I've ever heard. Yes, you might be able to hold down a job and maybe even have a successful career. Yes, you might attend social events and maintain friendships. Yes, you might seem completely "normal" and problem-free to those on the periphery. But the internal battle never stops. Your legs hurt from standing up at a picnic because you can't bring yourself to sit on the grass and get contaminated. You're at the party but you're so socially anxious that all you can think about is leaving and you don't actually talk to anyone. You arrive freshly showered to work with no one realizing how difficult it was for you to simply get out of bed, let alone get in the shower. It's exhausting. And knowing the toll this type of life can take, Jennifer poses this question: "Where do you want to invest your emotional energy? Because you can invest it in managing all of those symptoms, but usually that means there's not that much left over to invest in participating in your life in healthier ways." I personally think we all deserve more than simply getting by. That's why you bought this book in the first place. You want more. You want love! And you're entitled to having enough mental energy to achieve it.

The good news in all of this is that medication is available if you're interested and meet the necessary criteria. If you have clear-cut anxiety and/or depression, your general practitioner or gynecologist might be able to prescribe an SSRI without having to refer you to a specialist. (It would be more unlikely for them to diagnose you with and treat you for OCD.) But if the first medication doesn't work, it's best to see a psychiatrist to help you figure out the right prescription. It's also important, as Jennifer says, "to believe in the medication you're taking. You want to be able to have a positive association around it." She continues, "It's so interesting how differently people think about medication or side effects once they're no longer as anxious or obsessive or depressed, because all of those mood states color the lines and distort your perception. You maximize the negative and you minimize the positive. You see things as all or none." And this kind of rigid thinking can make people reluctant to try medication in the first place. But if you do make the decision to try medication, it helps to go into the process with an open mind and a curiosity about how medication can help. You are trying it to see if it works. It's not a lifelong commitment. It's an opportunity for self-improvement.

A lot of people—including past me—mistakenly think that if they start medication, they'll be stuck on it for the rest of their life. As Jennifer explains, "There's always an opportunity to reevaluate or to try to decrease or go off. It also isn't necessarily a bad thing to be on meds indefinitely. If that's what allows you to be your best self, why wouldn't you? People worry about long-term side effects of medication and I always counter that with, 'We don't actually know.' It's impossible to do a good study on this because there are so many confounding variables, but what we do know are the long-term side effects of anxiety and depression on your brain. You can wonder about the side effects of the medication, but it's also important to wonder about the side effects of *not* being on medication. At least being on medication buys you presumably decades or however long of a better internal emotional quality of life."

Although Jennifer is talking about medication here, I think you can apply a lot of her perspective to your approach to mental health in general. You do only have one internal life. You don't have to white-knuckle your way through it. You can try a new treatment approach—such as CBT, mindfulness, or SSRIs—just to see if it works. There is also the possibility of using herbal medication, although you'd want to do so with caution and a lot of research, since none are FDA approved. Regardless of what you end up exploring, you owe it to yourself to get better control of your symptoms. And I guarantee your romantic relationships will reap the benefits.

Before we wrap up with fancy bullet point takeaways, I want to make it clear that there is no such thing as a miracle pill. While medication helps me significantly, I still deal with OCD symptoms surrounding contamination and occasional bouts of depression. The difference is that my lows are no longer so low that I can't even imagine crawling back to stable ground. And my OCD doesn't interfere with my day-to-day life in an overwhelming way anymore. At least right now. As I've said before, life will always be a roller coaster. We just want it to make sure it's the old-school, wooden kind that doesn't flip you upside down four different times in sixty seconds.

If you do decide to try medication, or if you're already on it, it's important to remember that medication alone will never be enough when it comes to attending to your mental health. You will always have to do additional internal and behavioral work. If you can't afford traditional therapy, there are some cheaper resources worth checking out, like online therapy and group therapy. There is also a lot of literature and research out there that can help you better understand your symptoms and how to combat them. You can even find CBT-focused apps and a plethora of mindfulness resources right on your smartphone. Medication is just one avenue of treatment, and it's not necessary or right for everyone. But if you are feeling stuck or emotionally exhausted, try not to limit your potential growth due to misinformation or fear. That's unfair to yourself and to your (potential) partner.

Wahoo! We finally got to those fancy bullet points I teased earlier! Try to remember:

- Not everyone will experience side effects when on medication. Everyone's body reacts differently to each individual medication.

- Sexual side effects and weight gain are often long lasting. You have to decide the cost benefit.

- You can try out different medications until you find the right match.

- Hitting or maintaining your goal weight won't guarantee you happiness. Focus on loving yourself instead of the numbers on a scale.

- Confidence is sexy!

- You don't need to white-knuckle your way through life.

- You can be on medication short term or long term.

- Medication by itself is not enough. You need to combine it with other forms of treatment.

- Your partner should value your internal emotional quality of life over any potential side effects that might affect your sex life together.

- You only get one internal life. Do your best to make it a great one!

As a reward for completing this chapter and examining any pre-conceived notions surrounding medication, you now get to read all about my sex life! Enjoy! I'm going to go hide under a blanket!

CHAPTER SIX

WHAT'S SEX GOT TO DO WITH IT?

MEET THE EXPERTS:

- **Dr. Jessica O'Reilly** is a sexologist whose PhD research focused on sexual health education training for classroom teachers with an emphasis on healthy relationships, HIV/AIDS, and intersectionality. Her educational background includes courses in counseling skills, sex and disability, group therapy, equity studies, sexual development, resolving sexual concerns, and cognitive behavioral therapy. Jess is the author of five books, including *The Ultimate Guide to Seduction and Foreplay: Techniques and Strategies for Mind-Blowing Sex*; host of the *Sex with Dr. Jess* podcast; and she appears weekly in international media, from *Forbes* and *The Doctors* to *Cosmopolitan* and *Entertainment Tonight*. She hosted PlayboyTV's reality hit *Swing* and has facilitated couples retreats in more than forty-five countries, from Lebanon to Switzerland. We'll be referring to her as Jess.

- Remember **Dr. Zac Seidler** from chapters three *and* five? He's back! And we'll (still) be referring to him as Zac.

Note to the reader: While I have a complicated relationship with sex, I still identify as a sexual person. As such, I can't speak to the ace experience. But if you are ace, there are some great resources by asexual authors, including *Ace: What Asexuality Reveals About Desire, Society, and the Meaning of Sex* by Angela Chen. 10/10 would recommend!

have an unhealthy relationship with sex that continues to interfere with my happiness. Wow, that feels good—and terrifying—
to admit. Unlike other parts of my mental health that I've spent
years and thousands of dollars examining, I have kept this
aspect of my life buried deep inside of me. Whenever a flicker
of this issue pops up, I immediately hit it back down like a game of
Whac-A-Mole with no prize at the end. I have struggled with my
relationship to sex and my own sexual pleasure ever since I saw my
first penis on purpose (I saw my first penis *not* on purpose when it
was falling out of a random dad's swim shorts at a lake). But it took
me until this past year to finally use the term "unhealthy" while in a
therapy session. Using that specific word was an *aha* moment. For
maybe the first time, I understood the full weight of my baggage.
And let me tell you, it's oversized and far past the fifty-pound limit.

Everything about this book is vulnerable, but I've explored a lot
of the subject matter publicly in some way before. I never cared if
the whole world knew I was on antidepressants or went through
periods of self-harm. It's all a part of my journey and my experience, and I thought talking about it openly would maybe help other
people do the same. People have consistently told me I am "brave"

for sharing my deepest secrets online. What they don't realize is that it was *easy* for me to talk about that kind of stuff. It came naturally to me, and once I started, it was hard to stop. It seemed like my life was an open book. But no one knew it was missing a pretty hefty chapter! (This is that chapter, BTW! Very exciting!)

After years of shying away from discussing my sex life, I finally realized my relationship with sex is completely tied up in both my mental health *and* my dating history. To not include it here would be a disservice both to you, the reader, and to me, the ever-evolving person. That said, I didn't want to write this. While I've always been proactive in improving other aspects of my life, I have consistently evaded doing any real work in this area. I wonder if any of you feel the same? If so, why? Is it because we have had to work so hard to just get through the day that a satisfying sex life feels like a cherry on top of a sundae we don't deserve? Does dealing with our sexual issues feel like an unnecessary burden when we are constantly in triage for other, more urgent problems? Or is that just me?

In sharing the most intimate details about myself, I hope to accomplish four things:

1. Destigmatize sexual issues and open up the conversation around them

2. Help other people who have experienced something similar realize they are not alone

3. Highlight the connection between sex and mental health so they are no longer looked at as two distinct and separate issues

4. Encourage open communication between you and your partner(s) so we can all have the best sex of our lives!

And if none of that works, at least I will have succeeded in mortifying my parents! And with that: drumroll please . . . *bum bum ba da dum*.

For a long time, I thought my vagina was broken. Yes. Broken. Damaged. Ruined beyond repair. Why? Because it didn't work the way I was promised by pop culture. I had watched movies. I had listened to songs. I had read books. All of them exalted the physical pleasure of sexual acts. (Okay, maybe not all, but most!) Enjoying sex appeared to be one of the few things that tied humanity together. It was a rite of passage. A light at the end of a potentially mediocre tunnel of human existence. As for me, I thought it was a pivotal component of the thing I so desperately craved: a romantic relationship. But then I started having sex, and dread began to sink in. Something didn't feel right. And most of the time, I felt nothing at all.

Here's one of my more shameful confessions: I don't remember losing my virginity. Not because I was drunk or high, I simply don't remember it. This remains one of the weirder details of my life. Sure, I have a historically bad memory, but this feels especially bizarre. Luckily, I do remember *who* I lost it to: a twenty-four-year-old cop when I was eighteen. He was very nice to me during the brief period of time we dated, and I don't remember feeling pressured into it in any way. But then again, I don't remember much! Did I block it from my memory on purpose? Or was it so deeply disappointing that my brain thought, *Eh, we don't need to use up storage on this*? If the latter is true, then why do I still remember being bullied at summer camp for peeing naked? (I was wearing a one-piece. You have to pee naked when you're wearing a one-piece!)

As a result of my faulty retention, I don't know exactly when it started to bother me that I wasn't experiencing much of anything other than occasional pain during penetration. But I do know I realized at some point in college that my body wasn't reacting the way I had been promised. This was pretty upsetting, especially because I was sleeping with a bunch of people in the hope that one of them would grow to love me. As someone with anxiety, I immediately jumped to the worst possible explanation for my "sexual failing"— that my vagina was broken.

And that's where we arrive at my second shameful confession: When I was a little kid, I masturbated all the time. I didn't use my hands though. Instead, I would rub myself on the arm of a chair or a couch. I would do it while reading or finishing up homework. It wasn't so much a *sexual* experience for me as a purely physical one. As time went on, I learned to tone down my vocal response to it so no one would know what I was up to in the other room. Looking back now, I'm sure this is all fairly common and natural. But when I was eighteen and suddenly letting a partner touch my vagina for the first time, I was CONVINCED all my excessive masturbation had ruined or dulled my nerve endings and my vagina, to put it succinctly, was broken.

Despite my normal verbal diarrhea surrounding my other issues, this was not something I have *ever* wanted to talk about or admit. I secretly believed there was something physically wrong with me for a very long time. To be honest, a small part of me still does. I'm not sure where my shame around this part of my story comes from. Was it my excessive masturbation? Was it my stupidity in thinking excessive masturbation could ruin my clitoris? Or was it simply the potential embarrassment of being seen as a sexual person by people I wasn't actively sleeping with? I'm sure it's a lovely mixture of all three. Whatever the source, this shame kept me quiet, which only led to me feeling more defective and alone.

HOT TIP: Shame is a harmful emotion. Luckily, talking out loud about the things you're ashamed of can deflate their power. That's why I'm fighting my instincts and writing to you right now about my genitals. Yippee!

What I didn't understand at age eighteen, twenty, twenty-two, twenty-four . . . is how important your mindset is when it comes to sex. I was far too anxious as a late teen to simply lay back and be present in my first few sexual experiences. The anxious voice in my head didn't take breaks back then, and it certainly wasn't going to shut up while I was naked with a boy! Love is a battlefield, and I was across enemy lines! This wasn't some run-of-the-mill activity. I couldn't turn my brain off during such a crucial mission (i.e., forming physical intimacy that I hoped would quickly turn into emotional intimacy and then, you know, marriage!). This was a high-stakes situation! So that voice in my head was in overdrive: *Am I doing this right? Is he doing this right? Why does it feel like this? Why don't I feel anything? Will he still like me after? Will I still like me after? What if my parents call me right now . . . or right now?*

I'm sure I wasn't alone in overthinking during my formative sexual encounters. Unfortunately, my anxiety irrationally decided that these limited experiences proved a bigger point: There was something physically wrong with my body that made me unable to orgasm or feel any real pleasure alone or with a partner. And that is how it would be forever until I died, with absolutely no room for improvement. (This type of thinking is called catastrophizing. It's a tendency to blow situations out of proportion and imagine the *worst* possible outcome as the *only* possible outcome. An easy way to catch yourself catastrophizing is flagging the use of words like "never" or "always." For example: "I'll *never* be happy again." Or, "I'll *always* be alone on Valentine's Day." Catastrophizing is super destructive, and I personally think we should all put a dollar in a jar whenever we do it. And then spend that money on ice cream once we feel better and realize we overreacted.)

Anyway, back to catastrophizing my genitals. This wasn't just a "penetrative sex doesn't do it for me" type of thing. This was an "absolutely nothing does it for me, oh god, what is wrong with me" type of thing. Honestly, it all made sense to me at the time. Since I was already so broken mentally, why wouldn't my vagina be broken too? I was destined to be unhappy! Better to just accept it and move on. Right? (Wrong.)

For a long time, orgasming was not my priority. I had college classes and improv and my ever-present mission to lock down a man. Plus, I often had to struggle to find a will to live, which didn't leave much time to worry about the little things like sexual pleasure. I did bring it up occasionally over the years to test the waters. I remember briefly mentioning it to my first gynecologist, who wasn't (1) concerned, or (2) helpful. My psychiatrist at the time was a bit more receptive since antidepressants are notoriously problematic in this area. As we've discussed, it's extremely common for them to lower your sex drive and/or interfere with the ability to orgasm. So she added a prescription of Wellbutrin to whatever I was currently on. (Wellbutrin is often used to combat side effects of SSRIs, especially the sexual ones. *Harper's Bazaar* once published an article about it with the headline "The Happy, Sexy, Skinny, Pill?") I was hopeful that maybe this would be a quick solution to an ongoing problem! It wasn't. Which only further proved my thesis that the problem was physical and therefore unsolvable. (I was still ignorantly unaware of how people respond differently to medications. Mainly because I hadn't written chapter five of this book yet.)

Part of the problem with my inability to experience vaginal pleasure was that instead of it being an enjoyable activity, sex simply became a tool in my efforts to find someone to love/marry me. Ideally, people experience sexual desire and *then* have sex for pleasure. I had a sex drive, but I didn't always rely on it to guide me. If a boyfriend wanted to have sex, I'd have sex. How could they leave a girl who had sex all the time? It's not like it mattered if I was in the mood or not since the end result was always the same: me focusing exclusively on his pleasure. My sexual availability was just another weapon in my arsenal, along with my sense of humor and my parents' time-share in Mexico. In my mind, it added to my value as a potential partner that I was always down to bone whenever they wanted to. I was fun! I was game! I was completely selfless! That's why it was so very frustrating when sex suddenly became a huge problem in my relationships.

My lovely ex-boyfriend Lloyd was the first person to confront me about my sexual issues in my early twenties. Lloyd was ten years older than me, although I was incorrectly certain at the time that we had the same level of maturity. For our one-year anniversary, Lloyd presented me with a gift: a really fancy vibrator. Me, now, would be thrilled with this purchase. Me, then, freaked out and got scary-angry. I was unreasonably furious for a number of reasons. One of the stupider ones was realizing I couldn't brag about what my boyfriend bought me for our anniversary to my friends and family. I'm pretty sure I said, "What am I supposed to say if they ask? He got me a vibrator?!?!" (Yes, Allison. That's exactly what you say, and then patiently wait for the incoming high fives. Vibrators are dope.) But deep down, underneath my dramatics, I was mostly mad that he was acknowledging something I didn't want to: Our sex life wasn't perfect. And he wanted me to work on it. Not for him. But for me. What an asshole, right?! It's so much easier to ignore our problems!

As we all know by this point in the book, it's important to rationally listen when a partner points out a problem. But, if you're anything like twenty-three-year-old me, your first instinct is to shout, "Fuck you! I am the way that I am! Do NOT try to change me!" In some cases, this reaction is actually warranted. If, for example, your partner is suggesting a change to your physical appearance, such as a breast enhancement, scream your heart out. But most of the time, if you're in a healthy relationship, a partner will only high-light a concern because they think working on it will improve your personal happiness and/or your happiness as a couple. So listen to them. Take time to process what they're saying. And remember it's coming from a good place (hopefully!).

Following that anniversary gift was the first time I made my sexual issues a main topic in my therapy sessions. At this point I was no longer on medication and couldn't blame an SSRI for any muted sensations. My therapist, Sheri, tried to assure me that there was nothing physically wrong with my body and that my hang-ups were most likely, if not definitely, psychological. This confused me. I had no history of sexual abuse. Why would I have sexual hang-ups from the very beginning of my sexual journey? She, shockingly, pointed to my anxiety as the culprit. Oh, yes, my anxiety. It had already interfered in every other aspect of my life. Why wouldn't it interfere in the bedroom, too? Sheri thought the solution would come from getting me out of my own head and asked me to purchase a book of fantasies. It was basically a collection of short erotica aimed at the woman reader. Now, I freakin' love to read—ask anyone—but this felt dumb. It felt like homework. And for the first time in my life, I was certain I was going to fail an important assignment.

One of the biggest triggers for my anxiety is the possibility of something never happening. On the way to get my driver's license, I started to panic because I realized there was a world in which I might never pass the test and never drive. Life did not owe me a driver's license! I might live my whole life without one. (This was similar to my overwhelming fear regarding finding a partner and never being able to orgasm.) But, despite my existential worry, I managed to pass my driver's test on my first try. Fortunately, there are specific instructions to help you successfully drive an automatic car that can be taught by pretty much any person with a clipboard. Unfortunately, there is no such guide for affairs of the heart or the human body. Which is a huge bummer. Imagine if there were! I'd put my body in drive and orgasm all over town! (I took the metaphor too far. I'm sorry.)

Here's something you probably already know: Feeling stressed out about coming is a surefire way to make sure you don't come. I read the erotic book on and off and used the vibrator, but focusing so hard on this "flaw" only made me feel more defeated. Why should I spend all of my time and energy on something that would never happen anyway? Much better to ignore it and go through a painful breakup with Lloyd instead. (Unrelated but still devastating.) My life was a constant work in progress filled with anxiety, obsession, and ennui. I had so many other issues I needed to tackle with my limited energy before I could focus on sexual pleasure. So I did what I always did back then: Instead of turning inward and working on myself, I set out to find someone else to validate me.

Enter Match.com (who did not sponsor this book).

About eight long months after ending it with Lloyd, I signed up not just for online dating, but for *paid* online dating. Your girl was desperate, and I'm pretty sure so were my parents, because they offered to pay. Within a few days, I had matched with Tom. Tom was a thirty-two-year-old lawyer who drove a Porsche. This was all I needed to know to plan my engagement party. (Notice the use of "my" and not "our." Great priorities!) We hit it off, and within six weeks I had pressured him into making our budding relationship official. No gray areas allowed for Old Al!

And now we have arrived at the part of my story where I tell you a guy broke up with me because I couldn't orgasm. Sure, it was probably a bit more complicated than that, but this was my main takeaway. For almost the entire six months we were together, I was bursting with anxiety because I was dating someone who clearly didn't like me very much. It was obviously an unhealthy relationship, but he had a steady job in LA so I held on tight. I couldn't go back to being alone. It was too scary. Until we were suddenly "on a break" and I realized that was worse. There was not a minute during the week of our break where I was not obsessing over his impending decision. *Would we get back together? Would we not? Would I hear from him now? What about now?* It was excruciating and my lovely parents got to witness its physical effect on me while visiting LA. They really can't catch a break!

Tom finally called me while I was at an outdoor mall, which is a super fun setting to have your heart ripped out of your chest. I can't remember the specifics of the call, but he said something along the lines of, "I'm sure there will be guys who aren't bothered by you not orgasming. I'm just not one of them." The moment we hung up, after I had shamelessly begged him to reconsider, I started sobbing at a table with my mom. These people eating ice cream immediately came over and sat right next to us, which I still think is weird and borderline rude. I don't need a ton of privacy to publicly cry, but I at least appreciate the illusion of it. Normally I would never talk to my mom about my sex life, but that phone conversation was so raw and shocking that I couldn't stop myself from spilling. She lovingly listened while my dad made himself busy, probably buying a frozen banana. (The Raskins love frozen bananas.) Later, as I sobbed on my bed, my parents made me call my therapist. I was on the cusp of yet another love-induced breakdown. And I don't think I need to tell you this guy was not worth my tears.

For years afterward, I was traumatized by that breakup. Whenever I'd bring up my inability to fully orgasm with a friend, they would quickly assure me that it "doesn't matter" and wouldn't cause any real problems. That's when I'd hit them with, "A guy *dumped* me because of it!" (An easy, if devastating, way to win the argument.) I understand now that he is a piece of trash and I am much better off without him and his difficult-to-get-into Porsche. But the experience still scarred me. The subject I was already so sensitive about became even bigger in my head. I saw my own body as a huge red flag. That's why it made a lot of sense for me to start dating someone new only two weeks later. (JK JK—it was a horrible idea.)

I'll be the first to admit I had a pretty obvious dating pattern before my most recent relationship. I'd get involved with someone I put on a pedestal, obsess over locking them down, eventually push them away, and then immediately date someone else who put *me* on a pedestal so I could reclaim all the power and enjoy my ass being kissed until I realized I didn't respect them. It wasn't a good pattern, but I promised to be honest with you. So, following the trauma of Tom, I immediately got involved with James after he slid into my Facebook messages. James was a classic rebound who moved very quickly and wrote me long emails about how to improve our relationship, which lasted a total of four months. He was also determined to "fix me."

Your partner should never view your sexual issues as something that can be "fixed" or "solved." I think open communication is important, but the end goal should be connection and comfort, not a mind-blowing orgasm. While James repeatedly assured me it wasn't an issue that I couldn't come, his insistence on working on it proved otherwise. He made us try a practice called orgasmic meditation (OM) where I would lie on a pillow with my vagina in the air while he fingered me for *way* too long. According to the practice's website, "OM puts you in touch with your body and your sexuality. During the practice, one person strokes another person's clitoris for fifteen minutes with no goal other than to feel the sensation." While this is a lovely idea, it was fairly obvious that the end goal was an orgasm and not simply a "sensation" (although I would have been thrilled to have any sensation). Instead, I felt nothing other than a growing sense of resentment toward James. Once again, my sexuality felt like homework, which is the opposite of sexy.

It can be easy for those of us living with mental illness to look to our partners for help. We want to get better so desperately that we're often open to any and all suggestions. Oh, this nighttime tea helps you sleep? Great! Pour me a mug! CrossFit stopped your panic attacks? I'll try (one) class! The tricky part is figuring out when your partner is overstepping—when they are not just offering suggestions, but hoping to fix or solve you. If you get the sense that your partner is only planning to stay if you significantly change, you should be the one to leave. Even if they have a really cute dog.

After a few months of feeling like a science experiment, I eventually broke up with James over the phone while he was out of town because I, too, am capable of doing shitty things sometimes. My parents had to refund his plane tickets that had already been purchased for a Raskin family vacation, but my freedom was worth it. No one was making me lie on a pillow and concentrate on my clitoris for minutes on end anymore. I was back on the prowl, and two months later, I had a new guy and a new plan! (Don't worry about James. He's married now. I just pray she likes really long, emotional emails. And throw pillows.)

My new plan with my new guy involved something I had never tried before: faking it. I'd started seeing another guy named Tom. (Not his real name, but his real name was the same as the other guy, so I feel like I need to call him Tom, too. Or Tom 2. See what I did there?) I didn't think Tom 2 would turn into a real boyfriend, so I decided this was my time to experiment. Wouldn't everything go smoother if I just *pretended* to come? Also, it was pretty fun to fake it. We've all seen *When Harry Met Sally*. This was my diner scene. And he didn't even question it! Success! But then Tom 2 became my boyfriend for a year and a half. Despite my acting skills, I couldn't keep up the charade for *that* long, so I simply stopped faking. Tom 2 didn't seem to notice or care. It was business as usual, if your business is a somewhat toxic relationship that causes overwhelming and often debilitating anxiety. (He's the guy from the plane story at the beginning of the book! Surprise!)

At some point during our tumultuous relationship, the sex stuff caught up to me and I weepily confessed about my "dysfunction," as I saw it. Tom 2 sort of shrugged and said he knew I couldn't orgasm. He didn't seem bothered or want to talk about it. So I followed his lead and instead focused on his whereabouts at all times, since I was convinced he was going to cheat on me. He didn't, but we still broke up. (Thank god.) While other partners fixated on my sexual experience *too* much, Tom 2 cared too little. He was happy to get in and get out about once a week, my enjoyment be damned.

This is not a sign of a loving partner. There should be a middle ground where both people feel taken care of—whatever that means to you. Emphasis on "whatever." Everyone's preferences are totally different. Just scroll through PornHub for one minute if you don't believe me.

Right around my twenty-eighth birthday, after many failed relationships and zero progress on addressing my unhealthy relationship to sex, I dove headfirst into a serious relationship with Max. (Remember Max? The guy I broke up with in his therapist's office? That Max!) Max was not cool. Max was not confident. But Max made me feel safe. He never treated my sexual issues as something to fix and instead was always game to explore with me. If we stumbled upon something good, great! If not, who cares, we were still having sex and being intimate. Max was the first person I let focus on my vagina for an extended period of time. (Aside from that awful OM exercise, but I don't count that since it was clinical and torturous.) Letting someone down there was extremely hard for me. I felt vulnerable and afraid. What if I couldn't deliver? What if I disappointed them? What if I kept failing? My anxiety didn't realize the men I was sleeping with were thrilled to just *look* at a vagina. Any vagina. (I forgot to mention that in addition to all my other hang-ups, I was also convinced my vagina—or what I inaccurately called my vagina—looked disgusting because one lip is slightly longer than the other. For years, I fervently worried over that one centimeter only to later realize: NO ONE CARES IF YOUR LABIA ARE UNEVEN. All bodies are beautiful and all vulvas are normal! There is already so much hate in the world. Try not to direct any at your own genitals.)

Every time I've seen a storyline on-screen about a woman being unable to orgasm, it always ends with her orgasming. She's suddenly with the right guy or discovers a strange kink that works for her. It's already a taboo subject to cover. Heaven forbid it doesn't have a tidy happy ending. My story doesn't have one of those, but it does have progress. I discovered that in certain situations, I am able to reach a sort-of climax using my vibrator. I use the word "climax" lightly here. It's nothing to write home about, but it is something—a sort of dulled feeling that is vaguely reminiscent of those childhood orgasms. There is a buildup, if not an explosion. It is, at the very least, proof that my vagina is not broken. Also, I like it and it makes me feel good.

How did this happen, you ask? My best guess is that it had something to do with Max making me feel safe. I wasn't worried he was about to leave me or cheat on me with someone who could have multiple orgasms. Feeling safe is my anxiety's greatest adversary. When I feel safe, I feel more in control. I've learned that this feeling of safety is a crucial component in my ability to have a healthy relationship. Some of that safety comes from what my partner gives me, and some of that simply comes from a level of self-confidence where I know that no matter what happens in the relationship, I will be okay. I am stable enough to survive. And, after years of that not being the case, knowing that feels even greater than having a mind-blowing orgasm. (I assume.)

———

You might not realize it based on this entire chapter, but I *do* enjoy sex. I am allosexual, and I love physical intimacy. And aside from my vagina, I'm pretty responsive to touch. I also really enjoy giving my partner pleasure. Following my breakup with Max, I was determined to be open and direct with my partners about my relationship with my body and my ongoing journey to figure out what works for me. Despite my best intentions, this proved challenging because I often feel like a sexual imposter. Sure, I've *had* sex, but I've never experienced it the way I *thought* I was supposed to. You know that moment in *The 40-Year-Old Virgin* where Steve Carell says boobs feel like sand and everyone realizes he has no idea what he's talking about? I *felt* that moment. My OCD has always made me super uncomfortable with misleading people in any way. As a result, I've often felt that I can't openly talk about myself as a sexual person because I'm not experiencing sex the way I think I "should," and therefore I am a fraud who knows nothing. (Isn't mental illness fun?!)

Unlike for me, talking about sex comes easily to Dr. Jessica O'Reilly, a famous sex therapist who hosts a popular podcast aptly called *Sex with Dr. Jess.* She confirmed that anxiety can largely affect one's sexual desire, arousal, orgasm, and response, but sometimes a little bit of anxiety can be a good thing. It can make things more exciting when it's not out of control. But what happens when it is out of control or more prevalent than you would like? "If you're worried about having an orgasm, that worry activates the stress response instead of the relaxation response. The stress response impedes your ability to become physically and mentally aroused. You might not be able to get an erection. And an erection is a part of sexual response for all bodies—people with clitorises have clitoral erections and people with penises have penile erections," says Jess.

So what exactly do you do if your anxiety is getting in the way of a clitoral or penile erection? Jess suggests focusing on decreasing your anxiety overall, and not just in the bedroom. (She runs an online course called Mindful Sex that doesn't even mention sexual touch until ten sessions in.) She says it's important to first focus on pleasure in general: "I find that people need practice expressing pleasure—even just taking something delicious and eating it and letting their sounds and their breath and their moans and their movements emanate without inhibition. That's a really hard thing for most of us to do because we squash and we monitor and we prescribe expressions of pleasure, even when it comes to food! We're not allowed to eat with our mouths open and we're not allowed to let out 'mmm' or 'ahhh!' We are simply disallowed from those expressions. So I think [when] tackling or working through anxiety, that can be a really nice place to start. Just bring it back to pleasure, what feels nice in your body." I love this approach. For so long, I thought I was missing out on something important, when in reality I'm lucky enough to experience pleasure throughout the day! I'm guilty of moaning or humming without even realizing it when I eat something delicious. Why shouldn't devouring an ice cream sundae be as valuable an experience as multiple orgasms?

While the first step in changing our feelings and behavior is often changing our thoughts, it's not always that easy. Especially when you have a lot of damaging beliefs that need to be reframed. So midway through our call, I took a deep breath and explained my own history to Jess, asking her advice for someone who is convinced their body is broken. Her answer surprised me because it was both obvious and something I had never thought to consider: "We tend to get hung up on specific experiences, because in the absence of sexual health education that emphasizes pleasure, we know that most people turn to porn as their model of what sex should look like. If you compare your sexual response to an actor's sexual response, and you compare your sounds or your breath or your movements or your eyes rolling back in your head or an absence of that experience to someone who is performing an orgasm on the camera, I think we're all going to feel broken. We're all going to feel as though we're missing out." Holy fuck. She's right! I *was* comparing my own experiences to what I had seen portrayed not just in porn, but in the media in general. Who says people *need* to moan for sex to be good? Who says sex must include a performance worthy of an AVN Award*? (*It's like the Oscars for porn.) How would I have felt about my own sexual experiences if I went into them without any expectations? Probably a whole lot better! One of my friends often says, "I don't know how to describe sex, but I know when I'm having it." I love this sentiment. To me, this means sex can start with a kiss. And it can end without there ever being penetration.

Jess further elaborated on the ramifications of having a false idea of what sex should be: "I think we have to begin with the education around the fact that sex sometimes includes orgasms and sometimes it doesn't. Orgasms can be big and loud and feel earthshattering, and they can feel soothing and quiet and underscored by a sense of relief." At the end of the day, sex is going to look and feel different for everyone, but that doesn't make any version of it less valid. It's not about coming; it's about people entering a certain headspace together. I shouldn't feel like an imposter because I've never gripped a headboard in pure ecstasy.

So that has been my goal recently: figuring out how to get in the right headspace, despite my anxiety. But it can be difficult to tackle this sort of thing if you don't even know where to start. Especially if that not knowing only adds to your anxiety. So I turned to Jess for some guidance. She recommends asking yourself a series of questions to help you determine your sexual values. These questions include:

- What do I find challenging about sex?

- Why is sex important to me?

- What surprises me about sex?

- What is my sexual style?

- What does it mean to have a good sexual connection?

- What do I like about sex?

- When do I feel most in the mood for sex?

- When am I not in the mood for sex?

- How do I feel when I'm not in the mood for sex?

- How do I feel during sex?

(You can find more of these types of questions in Jess's book, *The Ultimate Guide to Seduction and Foreplay*, cowritten with Marla Renee Stewart. There are hundreds of them!) If you're anything like me, most of the answers will not come immediately. But that just means it's another great opportunity to take out your fancy notebook, put on some fancy music, and do some fancy thinking. I'll start. How do I, Allison Raskin, personally feel when I'm not in the mood for sex? Anxious and worried that I am going to have to have sex. This indicates that I need to become more comfortable telling my partner I'm not in the mood instead of just hoping and praying we will both fall asleep without it coming up! I'm learning how to say no so that when I do have sex, it is something I want and not something I'm doing simply to please someone else. I know that seems obvious, but it's a departure for me. I think it can be helpful for all of us to check in with ourselves before having sex to see why we are doing it. Is it something we truly want in the moment? Or do we feel like it's something we "should" do? The more "shoulds" we attach to sex, the less likely it will be a pleasurable and healthy experience.

It can take (a long) time to figure out what works for you. Sometimes I'm in the mood without any help other than being with my partner. Sometimes I want to watch porn or read something erotic. Sometimes I want to listen to music. But more often than not, I will turn to weed to help calm my anxiety and put me in the right mindset. I know this might be a controversial statement, especially for readers who don't live where it's legal, but it's my truth. Weed helps, so you know what? A lot of times my sexual activities involve weed and a vibrator. You get to determine what works best, and if it isn't hurting anyone and it's consensual, fucking go for it.

"The more 'shoulds' we attach to sex, the less likely it will be a pleasurable and healthy experience."

The final part of the complicated equation of sexual satisfaction + anxiety is adding another person(s)—if that is something you desire to do. While it can be hard to figure out what you like, it can be even harder to express what you like to someone else. Especially if you have sexual hang-ups like me or are on meds that lessen libido. I still find it excruciating to talk to a partner about sex. One of the reasons these conversations have historically been so hard for me is that the most common piece of advice is "tell your partner what you want," which (falsely) implies you've figured that part out!

That's why it's important to get a grasp on your sexual values. Once you've done that, you can start to clue your partner in to what you've learned about yourself. And by the way, this will all be easier to share if you are already having open and vulnerable conversations about everything, not just sex. If you've laid the groundwork for open communication, like we talked about in chapter four, the sex talk will be just another link in your growing connection. Knowledge is power, after all!

Before diving into the conversation, it's important to acknowledge that anxiety, depression, and other mental illnesses can get in the way of one's sex drive, resulting in a lot of shame and guilt. The best way to alleviate those feelings, according to Jess, is to be specific about what is going on. "You might say something like, 'I feel attracted to you and I want to feel close to you, but I'm just not in the mood for sex and here's why. What are some other ways we can stay connected? What would make you feel sexually fulfilled?'" she says. Take the pressure off yourself to constantly feel sexual, because it's a waste of time and potentially harmful to your self-confidence if it doesn't turn out to be true. You and your partner can find many ways to satisfyingly connect that don't have to include your genitals.

If you have difficulty orgasming or maintaining an erection, that's another important thing to share. While it might seem embarrassing to admit, in reality it's just another piece of information that will be helpful for your partner to know. Any understanding partner won't take it personally, and if they do, Jess says, "They sure are giving themselves a lot of credit. The person whose body is having the orgasm plays a much larger role than the person who is supposedly 'giving' an orgasm. If someone is taking something personally, they have to do the work. They have to figure out, *Why am I taking this personally? Where does this come from? What are my sexual experiences and values that have led me to arrive at this conclusion? Why is my sexual ego or sexual self-esteem so closely tied to my partner's performance of pleasure in a way that validates my own sexuality?* There's a lot to unpack there." Take that, Tom 1! You need to do the work, not me! (I mean, I still need to do a lot of work, just not on my ability to orgasm for Tom 1's pleasure and self-esteem.)

Zac also weighs in on sexual dysfunction: "I see a lot of guys who end up coming to me for premature ejaculation or erectile dysfunction. They believe it to be a physical situation, and it's very difficult to have conversations with them about the fact that it's purely anxiety based." But Zac actually sees the psychological cause as a *good* thing because it's something that can be directly addressed through psychotherapy: "I flip it on its head and I say, 'You know, this is great. This is something you can change with some hard work and without any form of serious intervention. So why do you see this as the worst option? This is the best option.'" This is a wonderful reframing, even if the idea of diving into your psyche might initially feel more ominous than simply taking Viagra.

Part of what makes these conversations around sex so charged and vulnerable is that many people think sexual satisfaction is a major indicator of the overall quality of a relationship. I asked Jess if this is true or just another harmful misconception. Her response was appropriately nuanced: "Sexual fulfillment absolutely can affect relationship fulfillment. But again, what does sexual fulfillment mean? Does it mean we have sex often? Sure, for some people. But other people are in very high-quality relationships that are sexless.

So yes, sexual fulfillment and relationship fulfillment can be positively correlated, but there is no one specific way to be sexually fulfilled." Basically, you and your partner need to be on the same page about what satisfies both of you without getting hung up on frequency or orgasm. A lot of sex does not always equal good sex. And a lot of orgasms does not necessarily equal fulfillment or connection. Focus on you, focus on your partner, and throw all societal expectations out the door. You're officially in charge of your own story, and no one else needs to read it.

If you still feel like you need outside help navigating all of this and/or discovering what works for you, consider seeing a sex therapist. Don't worry, this doesn't mean you will have to have sex in therapy. (I mistakenly thought this for a while.) It also doesn't need to be a massive undertaking. A lot of therapists these days will offer solutions in just one to three sessions. And, with certain open-minded therapists, you can state your goals from the beginning instead of having to do a deep dive into your entire sexual history. Jess recommends seeing a professional if "the same issues keep arising from relationship to relationship." We can't expect change if we don't try something new—and I'm not just talking about sex toys.

———

Wow! I did it. I wrote about my sex life openly and honestly. Was it liberating? Oh, yeah! Am I still embarrassed that people I know in real life will read this? Absolutely! But I pushed through the discomfort so we could get to the fun part: bullet points of what we've learned!

- A fulfilling sex life looks different for everyone and isn't limited to what you do or don't do with your genitals.

- Anxiety, depression, and other mental illnesses can absolutely get in the way of arousal, desire, and performance. That's okay! We just have to be open to talking about it so our partner(s) can understand what's going on.

- Before talking to your partner about sex, take the time to figure out your own sexual values.

- Practicing mindfulness *outside* of the bedroom can ultimately help you feel less anxious *in* the bedroom.

- Pressure is a major buzzkill! Don't put pressure on yourself and don't put pressure on your partner.

- Focus on pleasure in general instead of fixating on climaxing. Also, moan when you eat. I really recommend it!

- If your partner takes your inability to orgasm personally, that is their problem, not yours. (*Cough, cough,* Tom 1.)

- We often have unrealistic expectations of what sex should look and feel like based on porn and media. Of course we are going to feel like we are missing out if we compare our natural responses to professional performances.

- Don't judge your genitals. Looking at you, my slightly uneven labia!

I still have a lot of work to do in this area of my life, but I think that's okay. Just because I'm doing so much better overall doesn't mean I've figured everything out. I'm still very much in the middle of my journey—much like we are in the middle of this book! Let's keep going!

CHAPTER SEVEN

HOW DO I DATE PRODUCTIVELY?

y therapist once described dating as a job where you are looking for the best candidate, and my brain exploded (in a good way). I had never thought of my search for a life partner so clearly and succinctly before. While I've always utilized my type A personality in other areas of my life, dating was supposed to be different, right? I was supposed to follow my heart and not my

methodical mind. *If it's meant to be, it will be. Love will find you when you stop looking. Everything happens for a reason!* These sayings are all well and good if you're looking to embroider an inspiring pillow for your grandma, but are they actually true? Would you apply the same thought process to any other aspect of your life? Imagine if someone told you, "You'll find a meaningful career the moment you stop looking!" Uh . . . what? How, exactly? Much like you can't build a meaningful career without, you know, working, you can't find a partner without dating! The tricky part is figuring out how to date in a way that serves you and respects your time. No one wants to waste their emotions or $14 on a first-date cocktail any more than they have to. (Personally, I prefer an ice cream first date, but then again, if I could add ice cream to any situation, I would.)

For the purpose of this chapter, we're going to assume that you have put in the hard work, reached a comfortable level of emotional stability, and are officially ready to dive deep into that sweet, sweet dating pool. Now we just have to figure out how to not drown in all the possibilities and endless texting! Luckily, I asked two professional dating coaches for their advice on how to make the dating process more productive and less soul-sucking. I'm also going to throw in some of the best tips and tricks I've personally developed over the years. You will definitely want to get your notebooks ready, and maybe think about getting a laminating machine. Imagine the sheer power of being able to laminate in your own home!

Let me introduce you to our dating experts. Devyn Simone is a celebrity matchmaker and dating expert who works with the matchmaking company Three Day Rule. Nick Notas is a dating and confidence coach who works mostly with men through his own consulting business. Despite Devyn and Nick's different backgrounds and genders, I found a lot of overlap in their advice. Plus, they were both incredibly nice when I randomly reached out and begged for an interview. (Thanks again!)

Since we're talking about dating in the twenty-first century, I want to begin with a discussion about—you guessed it—online dating. Even though we've come a long way in the last few years, there is still a bit of stigma attached to this method of dating. And you know what I think about stigma! I hate it! Plus, I genuinely think online dating is awesome. The cold hard truth is that, as an adult, it's often difficult to find and connect with someone outside your preexisting social circle or your workplace. And while both options are convenient, they can sometimes lead to disaster. Dating online allows you to interact with people you wouldn't have crossed paths with otherwise. Maybe your future partner is an astronaut! That would be so cool for you!

Another huge advantage of online dating is that it allows you to be upfront about your intentions. We've all met someone at a bar or party and wondered, *Are they single? Are they looking to date? Do they love dogs or only* like *dogs?!?!* While my social skills training has taught me that it's impolite to grill a random stranger about every intimate detail of their life, the same rules do not apply when you meet someone on a dating app. For starters, you're on a dating app, so it's safe to assume everyone is single and ready to mingle. (Unless their profile says otherwise and features a picture of their spouse.) But the differences between online dating and meeting a potential partner IRL are even deeper than that. Online dating allows you to explicitly state what you are and are not looking for without breaking societal norms. Deciding to match with someone online is the first step in a process of elimination to figure out if you are compatible enough to meet IRL. And in order to make that process as effective as possible, it's better for everyone to be open and honest from the get-go. Unfortunately, not everyone is going to be as open and honest as you will be after reading this chapter. But it's still important for you to set that gold standard by representing yourself correctly.

Both Devyn and Nick agree that honest representation starts with your picture selection. And luckily, they don't mean using glam shots in which you look your absolute best from every possible angle. Instead, think of it more like the old saying "A picture is worth a thousand words." Devyn elaborates, "You really want the pictures to fill in the blanks of your profile. The person looking at your profile should get a sense of what life would possibly look like with you. So, if in all your photos you are in really dark colors in your house with really dim lighting, it subconsciously sends the message that life with you might be a little dull." Now, maybe this *is* an accurate representation if all you do is sit in your house, in the dark, staring at the wall. But if you enjoy anything else, think about ways to showcase those parts of your life in your profile. And I'm not talking about that one time you tried fly-fishing five years ago. I'm talking about your everyday life. This could mean a photo of you reading your favorite book in the park, walking your dog, or playing tennis with your dad. (Are these examples taken directly from my life? Maybe!)

The other big aspect to keep in mind is the quality of your photos. Again, I'm not talking about the quality of your facial features or abdominal muscles. It's more about the resolution being clear enough that you are visible to the human eye. Devyn and Nick both recommend snapping your photos outside to take advantage of natural light. (Magic hour—right before sunset—has magic in the description for a reason!) Nick also points out that appearing well put-together in your outdoor, nicely lit photos sends the message that you take care of yourself both mentally and physically. As in, "I spent the time brushing my hair and matching my socks because self-care is important to me and I respect myself." Nick admits that when it comes to your profile photos, "they're marketing a story. In one way, it stresses out a lot of people that they have to focus on starting with good photos, but if you think about it more like, 'I just have to present

> "I've learned to never pretend to be someone I'm not—especially when dating."

what I want people to know about me' and come from a place of authenticity, then they will resonate with the right people."

Notice how Nick mentions "the right people." I'm not sure if you've noticed, but I have a pretty strong personality. I also have a razor-sharp sense of humor that some people may or may not find "extremely off-putting." But I've learned to never pretend to be someone I'm not—especially when dating. What's the freakin' point?! If you're not going to find my jokes funny over Hinge, you're certainly not going to find them funny thirty minutes into a dinner with no escape in sight. I often use my sense of humor as a barometer for my compatibility with people. If I can't laugh with someone, I pretty much don't want to do anything else with them either. There is no point in misrepresenting yourself just to land another date that ultimately won't go anywhere. That's the opposite of dating productively.

I'll be the first to admit that most people aren't able to open up as quickly as I am, especially over text. (Opening up in any way, even over a screen, requires a certain level of emotional vulnerability that might make your skin crawl.) Sometimes figuring out what to say in that initial message seems so daunting, you'd rather put your phone down or, more likely, stay on your phone, but switch over to Twitter. Luckily, Devyn has some tips for how to initiate a conversation that will last longer than you both just saying "hey!" ad infinitum until someone dies from natural causes and/or boredom. The most obvious approach is referencing something specific in the person's profile. For example, "I've read that book!" or "I also love to play tennis with my dad!" And if there is nothing to reference because the person's profile is devoid of personality and their photos don't reveal anything about their day-to-day life, Devyn says, "That's not someone to contact anyway, because you're not getting the full story. Either they haven't put in a lot of effort to open up and share or they're hiding something." Now, some of you might feel compelled to uncover whatever it is that they are hiding, but resist that urge and listen to a true crime podcast instead.

Devyn's other tried-and-true method for starting an actual conversation is mentioning something in pop culture. For example, if you are somehow transported back to April 2020, when ESPN Films and Netflix's *The Last Dance* ruled the internet, your first message might be something as simple as "Was Michael Jordan the greatest basketball player of all time? Yes or yes?" The pop culture reference is a great way to get to know someone's vibe and worldview before deep diving into the personal stuff. It's also a useful reminder that you are just two people chatting about a TV show or movie over a dating app, aka a pretty low-stakes scenario! It can be helpful to consider it from this perspective if you usually think of "dating" as something huge and anxiety-provoking. Sometimes it's just a little banter about a basketball team from the '90s! I don't even care about sports and I still wanted to talk about that documentary!

Some of you might be convinced that even with these suggestions, you are just absolutely, without a doubt, horrible at dating. It's part of your identity, for god's sake! Everyone knows you're horrendous at dating— that's your thing! You're single and miserable! The idea that dating could be something fun and potentially even successful seems as realistic as walking on water or agreeing with your homophobic uncle on anything. It's just not possible! Or is it? Nick has worked with many clients who think they're irrevocably lacking in this sphere of life. Speaking from years of experience, Nick says, "Nobody is the same and you can't figure people out like a math problem, but I think there are fundamental concepts about human connection and skills that anybody can learn once they understand what they are. If you can learn how to be good at your job or how to network in business or how to play the guitar, it's the same thing." Notice how he also compares dating to other parts of life instead of treating it like a magical unicorn that operates under separate rules in a faraway kingdom. The more we can approach dating like we approach the rest of human existence, the better off we will be and the less baffling it will feel.

I feel compelled to point out that interpersonal skills are vastly more difficult for some to learn than others, based on a whole host of factors, including neurodiversity and past trauma. But that

"The more we can approach dating like we approach the rest of human existence, the better off we will be and the less baffling it will feel."

doesn't mean you can't make some real progress, regardless of your starting point. One successful way to form a deeper connection is by pushing past surface-level information dumping and actually sharing your inner motivations. Nick explains, "If I'm opening up to somebody, I have to dig into more than the facts and the data of my job. I have to express my emotions and experiences behind it. Why do I do it? Why do I love it? What drives me? That's what starts to bridge you from 'This is just text on a screen' to 'Wow, I really feel this person, I feel their vulnerability.'" While exposing your internal workings to a stranger might seem terrifying, the more often you do it, the more natural it will feel and the quicker you'll feel comfortable opening up. Think of it as exposure therapy. In order to get over your discomfort, you have to repeatedly expose yourself to the very discomfort you want to avoid.

If, despite this advice, it still seems impossible to genuinely connect with someone exclusively over text messages, you're onto something! Nick says, "Texting is a poor means to make a connection. It's a great way to start one, but I don't think it's a great way to deepen or explore one." That's why he suggests moving away from texting as quickly as possible after matching on an app. Initiate a phone call, FaceTime, or IRL date so you and your date feel naturally compelled to open up more without a screen to hide behind.

But if you find that you have to text at the beginning—due to anything from conflicting schedules to their style of communication—try to have *fun* while you're doing it. I know this might seem like a foreign concept, especially if you have anxiety about dating, but hear me out. Actually, hear Nick out because he makes some great points. For starters, you never want to try to read someone else's mind and make assumptions about what they do or don't like to talk about. Not only is that the opposite of fun, it's a complete waste of time and also impossible. Instead, Nick says, you want to strive to "understand yourself better and write your messages from that standpoint. *How do I have the most fun right now? How do I self-amuse? What are the topics I would really be fascinated by?* You don't want to sound selfish or like it's all about you, but when you're seeing some text on a screen, you have no idea who the other person is. So it's best to start from a place of honesty. *Here are the jokes I like. Here's the kind of conversation I want to have. Here are the conversations that fascinate me.* The other person will see you are showing up more authentically. Therefore, they can show up more authentically." This fun-first approach also lets you get a sense early on if you are actually vibing with this person or not. For example, when you share your obsession with the Mamma Mia movie franchise, do they simply dismiss your taste, or do they lean in and ask why *Mamma Mia! Here We Go Again* is the best sequel of all time? (Again, this example might be too specific to me.)

The core truth of this advice extends beyond texting and online dating. You want to be yourself and initiate meaningful communication regardless of whether you meet on an app or at Trader Joe's. While I know it feels like conflicting information to tell you to treat dating like a job *and* have fun doing it, I think it's possible to have a combination of both mentalities. This is yet another situation where you can positively influence your experience by simply picking the right mindset. If you only associate the idea of dating with negative emotions, guess what you're going to feel when you're actually dating? Negative emotions! Instead, try to think of each new date as a learning opportunity, both about yourself and your potential partner. I'm not saying you have to make out with everyone you find vaguely attractive, but I will say that every failed relationship gave me better insight into what does and does not work for me. Your mental approach to dating will greatly influence your behavior on a date and your overall well-being as you think about, plan, and prepare for said date. And even if you have a positive attitude but it's still a total bust, maybe you'll get a funny story out of it to share at parties! People love to hear funny stories at parties. (I clearly go to a lot of parties, so I know.)

Let's assume for a moment that you've figured out how to match, text, and banter like a pro. How the heck do you figure out who is the right person for you to date long term? I've been preaching the value of self-awareness throughout this book, and you'd better believe I'm not going to stop now. In the same way that it's a bad idea to go into a grocery store without a list, you don't want to go on a date without some inkling of what (and who) you are looking for. Devyn agrees: "You need to prioritize your must-haves versus deal-breakers. You can't have an exhaustive list, but it's also not good to have no list, where it's like, 'Sure, I'll date him and her and him and her.' In that case, there is no baseline. Your future partner is going to be the VP of your life and you have no job requirements." You know how much I freakin' love a metaphor, and thinking of your partner as the "VP of your life" might just be my new favorite one. It not only highlights how important this person is, but also reiterates the fact that you are building a *life* with someone, and that is no easy task. You want to pick someone who will help you achieve your policies (goals) and not someone who is running a completely different campaign (lifestyle). (That was so fun for me!)

One of the easiest ways to spot any incompatibility red flags right out of the gate is to briefly (and I mean briefly) google your potential paramour. Why waste your time if one quick glance at their Twitter profile shows an affinity for the alt-right or a history of sexist jokes? As Devyn says, "Google is your friend. You're not going to get points for figuring it out on your own." The preemptive internet search before meeting up in real life can also give you a baseline for how this person chooses to present themselves to the world. Do you find it intolerable and narcissistic that they post fifteen Instagram stories a day? Better to know now, before they expect you to follow them. Or maybe they have a minimal internet footprint while you're a social media aficionado. Learning this ahead of time might lead you to have an important discussion about whether they're going to respect how you choose to spend your time. Just because you have different approaches to social media doesn't automatically mean you are incompatible. But you do need to at least understand and appreciate how the person you're dating operates so it doesn't come as a shock later if they don't post a romantic photo of you on Valentine's Day because they haven't posted a single photo in four years.

Once you've done your surface-level analysis, it's time to get into the deeper, more meaningful stuff through actual conversation. But how quickly can you expect to get to know someone? While every blossoming relationship has its own timeline, I think if you're looking for something serious, it's best to cover the important stuff on your first date. For me, that means: What is this person looking for? What are their values? What are their politics? How many dogs would they be willing to adopt? As Nick says, "It doesn't mean you have to have all the same interests and hobbies, but do this person's values resonate with you? Do you appreciate them? Do you respect their perspective and who they are?" For example, I'm someone who super prioritizes my family. Some people might find it strange that I call my mom multiple times a day. Luckily, those are the people I am never going to marry. I need to be with someone who values that part of my life instead of judging it. Plus, my mom is freakin' awesome.

Another great approach to assessing long-term compatibility with someone is to get a sense of their vision for their life. Devyn explains, "Does this person want to go and live on a remote island in five years? Does this person want to adopt forty-nine kids and have six of their own? Neither is bad! But if one wants to go live on the island studying trees, that might be a very different vision from yours. You don't need to go any further." So even if your day-to-day lines up right now, it's crucial to know what their ultimate aspirations are. Devyn says, "You can overlap in terms of compatibility, but if you have two distinctly different plans for your life, it's not going to work out well for you." If you don't have a clear vision for your life right now, that's important to share, too. Your potential partner might see this as adaptable and therefore compatible, or they might want to be with someone who shares similar clear goals.

I know it's easy to maintain all these hard-and-fast rules when your incompatible date is just a hypothetical, but what happens when they're a real person and you have a real spark? Unfortunately, if you're looking for a long-term relationship, you probably need to ignore that spark and think with your head. Devyn points out that sometimes people "don't like dating or have anxiety dating, so they'd rather get it over with and be in a relationship. And that's how you end up doing more harm than good." While I certainly understand the overwhelming desire to not be alone, dating productively means thinking big picture. And while this book is meant to provide you with tools to date successfully, it's also meant to help prevent you from dating unproductively and subsequently causing yourself (avoidable) heartache and pain. If you notice major incompatibilities and/or red flags at the beginning, I want you to write them all down over and over again in that notebook I made you buy until your hand hurts so much you realize it's better to cut ties. Or you can just walk away immediately and save a lot of time/ink. Totally up to you!

On the equally frustrating flip side of all this, sometimes you'll meet someone and you'll be completely compatible, except you're not sure if there is a spark. You *want* to be into them, but you don't know if you actually are on a sexual or romantic level. When I asked Nick and Devyn if it's possible for attraction to grow, they had somewhat conflicting answers. Devyn thinks that *some* people are capable of becoming more attracted over time, while others . . . not so much. Nick is even less optimistic: "For the vast majority, we know pretty quickly. It doesn't mean, 'Yes, I'm going to be committed,' or 'I'm head over heels attracted.' But I think most people know instinctively very quickly." He further explains, "Attraction is an emotional response. We don't choose it. We don't say, 'I want to be attracted to this person.' We just feel it. I think the thing that makes romantic relationships different is that intimate connection. And if that's not even remotely there, then a big part of the connection is missing."

Do I personally agree with this outlook? Yes and no. People's sexualities are too diverse and complicated to apply a one-size-fits-all rule or even loose guidelines. There are plenty of people, known as demisexuals, who are only sexually attracted to people *after* they get to know them emotionally. There are also people whose initial reaction will never change, regardless of how wonderful the other person is and how much time they spend together. And there are many more people who fall somewhere in between. What's important to figure out is how attraction works for *you*. If you're someone who, historically, has developed sexual and/or romantic feelings for someone after not originally feeling that way, it's worth waiting it out a bit to see if things change. But if you're more like me, and your attraction to someone has never grown over time, you shouldn't string the other person along by hoping a light will suddenly switch on. And if you don't yet have enough experience to know which way you lean, give it some time, but make sure you are keeping things casual and not leading anyone on. Because as much as we don't want to get hurt, we also want to avoid hurting other people.

Speaking of hurting other people, this wouldn't be an accurate chapter on modern dating if we didn't tackle ghosting. Cue the spooky music! Ghosting is one of contemporary society's most frustrating and anxiety-producing phenomena. It's also mean and inexcusable, IMHO. (The only exception is when you've already tried to break something off and the person continues to contact you and/or you feel threatened or unsafe in any way.) Not to sound like a broken record with a penchant for psychology, but ghosting is particularly harmful because it plays into our fears and anxiety surrounding the unknown. When someone doesn't explain *why* they don't want to talk to you anymore, it's basically an all-you-can-eat buffet for your brain to come up with every possible reason under the sun to explain why you suck and no one likes you. And these explanations are completely devoid of facts, because you don't *have* any facts, making your thoughts and assumptions even more dangerous and damaging.

Let's pretend you just got ghosted. How the hell do you handle it in a healthy way? Devyn says, "If you suspect someone is ghosting you, make up a story in your head—maybe an alien came and got them, whatever story makes you feel better—and then just let it go and move on. You cannot give other people the power to give you closure, because often they won't give it to you, and then you're left wondering or hanging on to something. Sometimes you won't get closure and you won't know why. And that's okay. Eventually you want to move forward anyway." As an alien enthusiast, I love this advice and urge all of you to assume benevolent alien abduction if someone you're seeing suddenly stops responding.

Devyn's other piece of advice, although less paranormal, is equally important. Just because you *want* an explanation and/or closure, doesn't mean you *need* an explanation and/or closure. Despite what your brain is telling you, you can continue to function and flourish without it. You also shouldn't take getting ghosted personally because, according to Devyn, it's just a reality of dating in the twenty-first century: "It happens to pretty much anyone. If they say it didn't happen to them, they either didn't date a lot or they're lying. Consider it a blessing or a gift, and move on to someone even better." Try to remember that anyone who ghosts you is too immature and lacking in communication skills to be worth your time anyway.

Some of you might be sweating a bit right now because you may or may not have ghosted people in the past. Don't worry, this doesn't automatically make you a horrible person. Your past is your past and this book is all about changing bad habits and patterns. While you can't take those actions (or your lack of action) back, you can commit to a ghost-free future. Maybe take a moment right now to write a contract with yourself in which you promise to never ghost anyone else ever again. You can even stipulate some sort of fine you'll have to pay if you break the contract. Might I recommend $200 to the NRA so you will never, *ever* want to pay it?

Even though I despise ghosting, I understand that breaking something off can be anxiety inducing and oftentimes it seems kinder to say nothing at all and seemingly disappear into the ether. Unfortunately, not replying is never the kind choice. As Nick puts it, "You make someone feel like you don't respect them enough as a human being to let them know how you feel. And it really sucks. It ends up being more combative and argumentative when you ghost." I love when the experts agree with me!

So what (the fuck) should you say if you want to break it off? It's not like it's a full-blown relationship—you've probably only met up once or twice, or maybe you haven't even met up yet! All you know is that whatever you have is not something you want to continue. Both Devyn and Nick agree that honesty is the way to go, even if it feels extremely uncomfortable in the moment. Devyn says, "Lies are tough. Especially when it's like, 'Oh, I'm not ready to date,' because you better believe that person is going to be keeping an eye out. The minute they see you in a relationship, they're going to be like, 'That person lied!' It can send them into a spiral." I am 100 percent guilty of lying to potential paramours. My favorite go-to lie was, "I'm getting back together with my ex." For some reason I thought this was the kindest explanation, because how can someone possibly compete with a shared history between two people? And clearly an elaborate ruse is better than, I don't know, simple honesty? Listen, we all make mistakes.

When explaining your reasoning for not wanting to see someone anymore, make sure you don't leave any wiggle room. Nick says, "If you obscure your truth at all—some people say 'I'm just not looking to date right now' or 'Maybe we can be friends and who knows what will happen'—then the other person often thinks there is a chance. Being honest and compassionately direct is saying something like, 'Listen, I had a lot of fun on our date, but I just don't feel that spark with you.' Or, 'Thank you for a wonderful evening, but I just don't feel like we're compatible.'" Nick admits, "We don't want that answer. But in thirteen years of doing this, it's the most effective, most healthy. 'I'm not rejecting you because I think you're so awful for me. I just didn't feel it. I wish you the best.'" Devyn adds that when you're open and direct in this way, "you're letting the other person know, 'I think you're great and I'm doing this not just for me but also for you.'" To put it simply, that person deserves someone who wants to show up for them, and you've realized you're not that person. Stringing them along will only prevent them from moving forward and finding their right fit. And we all deserve someone who is freakin' jazzed to be with us.

Now what if you've met someone new and you're not yet *jazzed* but you are intrigued? Is it a good strategy to play the field a bit, or is your energy better spent focusing on one person at a time? Devyn had some strong (and valid) opinions when I brought this up: "Do not put all of your eggs in one basket! I support the roster method, particularly if you're anxious, because your anxiety will put undue pressure on one relationship. Even if the relationship is 'meant to be.'" Unlike me, some people are able to casually date one person without thinking too much about it. It's just a new activity to add to their week. If you have anxiety, on the other hand, starting to see someone new, even casually, might feel like a constant itch in your brain that you need to scratch. *Are we talking enough? Are we talking too much? Will my family like them? Am I blowing this whole thing? Are they?!* Dating multiple people at once takes the pressure off and makes the entire experience less high stakes because no one person is your only option. Plus, Devyn says, "Having multiple options creates a more balanced perspective. I don't mean other options like leading people on, but like interviewing multiple candidates. What will happen sometimes, too, when having multiple options in the beginning, is you'll get a gauge of people's level of effort." For example, you might overlook someone canceling on you multiple times if their behavior is your only point of reference. But if you're also seeing someone else who always sticks to your plans and shows up on time, you'll realize that's the type of treatment you want and deserve, regardless of whether or not that person is who you want to settle down with.

Nick points out that without the experience of dating at least a few different people in your adult life, "it's hard to know if you're honestly evaluating the person in front of you, or if you're coming from a place of fear of not wanting to be alone." But, Nick adds, if you've had enough dating experience and you find dating multiple people at once to be anxiety inducing, it's perfectly fine to focus on one person at a time. (So long as you don't settle for the first person you happen to match with because dating is tiring and it feels easier to be done.)

Ultimately, if you do choose to date multiple people at once but you eventually want a monogamous relationship, the goal is to narrow your candidates down. Hopefully this is something that will happen naturally. Devyn explains, "Over time—and time could just be a matter of weeks—you start to ask yourself, *Who would I rather spend more time with?* And if there's a person you would rather spend more time with and you share the same vision, then you can let go of the others. Politely." By being—say it with me now—compassionately direct!

Despite the perks, dating multiple people at once can be messy. It's one thing to go on a few dinner dates with different people. That's simple. That's easy. But things become more complicated once sex is involved. It can help to have some clear-cut guidelines ahead of time, so you don't suddenly find yourself sleeping with three different people who all assume you're monogamous even though you haven't talked about it yet. The first step in establishing those guidelines is figuring out your relationship to sex and what works for you. (You can refer back to chapter six for some tips on how to do this.) For example, you might choose to make out with multiple people, but only remove your pants once you are monogamous. Or you might think it's important to have sex before committing to someone, to see how compatible you are in the bedroom. There is no wrong answer here because you are simply establishing your boundaries and your preferences.

The harder part is then taking this information and openly sharing it with everyone you're dating. Before things turn physical, it's your responsibility to clue your potential partner in to how you approach sex and physical intimacy. If you're (hopefully) safely sleeping with other people or open to sleeping with other people, you need to tell them that. If you're only comfortable having sex once you're in a committed relationship, you need to tell them. (Another friendly reminder that our definition of sex is not exclusive to penetration and includes many forms of physical intimacy!) This kind of direct communication might seem foreign and/or terrifying, but it's actually a sign of maturity and mutual respect. The golden rule is that you want to make sure your potential partners and even casual hookups are presented with all the relevant facts, so they can make an informed decision. That way they don't feel tricked or duped, and you can explore different relationships without feeling guilty or like you need to hide anything. Plus, initiating that conversation means you can ask the same of them. Are they hooking up with other people? Or are they just seeing you? The more openness—on both sides—the better.

A few years ago, I fell hard for a fellow writer. On our second date, I found out (exclusively through my intuition and direct line of questioning) that he was also dating someone else. This didn't sit right with me. I wanted to feel like we were both giving our connection a fair chance. It didn't mean we had to jump to becoming girlfriend and boyfriend, but I wanted us to focus on each other for a period of time in order to figure things out. He disagreed and didn't want to stop seeing other people, so we stopped seeing each other. Our boundaries didn't align, which proved that we didn't either. Cue that famous saying about trying to stick a square peg in a round hole. A few months later, I matched with someone (who is now my most recent ex) and we stopped seeing other people pretty immediately after that. We were on the same page from the beginning, which was a lovely relief. It's always going to be easier when your natural desires line up instead of trying to force someone to change. Also, you might not even know you're a circle talking to a square if you don't have those frank, potentially uncomfortable discussions at the beginning. And then it's suddenly three months later and you're trying to jam yourselves together to no avail.

Even if you're feeling steady and balanced when you start or reenter the dating process, all of the uncertainty and vulnerability that comes with it has the potential to knock anyone off course. That's why it's important to not lose track of your self-care in between all your matches, dates, and googling. When I asked Devyn what people should prioritize while dating, she immediately replied, "Your own well-being. You don't have to have it all figured out. You don't have to be perfect. Your partner's not going to care or even want you to be perfect. But you do need to make sure you're creating space to care for yourself. Whatever that is. Little things you enjoy. Having a hobby you love. Unwinding at the end of the week. You need to have already incorporated that into your routine or start doing that and keep doing that so you can stay in the best emotional and mental state possible." Despite the fact that you're actively searching for another person to share your life with, you, and you alone, need to remain your priority. Make sure you are taking time to recharge

"Despite the fact that you're actively searching for another person to share your life with, you, and you alone, need to remain your priority."

and not completely abandoning your established routine. This remains true even if your new paramour wants to hang out 24/7 or you have so many matches you could easily schedule six first dates a week. Don't let this one part of your life consume you. You've fought too hard to become someone you like just to lose yourself in another person.

Another strategy that really helped me when I was anxiously dating was deciding not to talk about my dating life. As a huge fan of therapy, this might sound weird and hypocritical, so let me explain my reasoning. My love life has always been my biggest obsession. In the past, whenever I was single or in that murky stage with someone, my mind was a constant loop of *Is this person going to love me or will I die alone?* It's honestly incredible that I was able to accomplish anything in between these obsessive thoughts. Add in all the time I spent analyzing every text and date with my friends, and it's a miracle that I remembered to eat. (JK, I always make time to eat.) Every time I talked to a friend about dating, it breathed more life into my obsession. Not only was *I* overly invested in the outcome, but I also had a small audience eagerly awaiting updates, or at least pretending to out of kindness. On the surface, I was simply a single woman discussing my dating life with my friends. In reality, I was an addict looking for people to enable my addiction and fuel my flames. Once I realized how much these conversations fed my spirals, I decided to go cold turkey. I even called it a "moratorium" because I love to be dramatic.

My moratorium on talking about dating lasted less than a week—old habits die hard—but it taught me some important lessons. For starters, my hypothesis was correct: By not analyzing and dissecting every little thing with someone else, my brain was less inclined to do so solo. During that time, I went on a first date without anyone knowing and it caused me far less stress than it would have otherwise. Also, when you tell the people in your life that you're instituting a moratorium on talking about dating to combat your anxiety, they will simply stop asking you about it! (Assuming they respect you and the concept of boundaries.) This cuts any potential conversation off at the start and lets you connect with friends about other things. You're still putting yourself out there and meeting new people, but you're not letting it consume the rest of your life. While the complete moratorium was extreme and difficult to abide by, I think it's worth making a conscious decision to talk less about your dating life if you're prone to anxiety or obsessive thoughts. Instead of sending your latest match's Instagram profile to everyone you know, just scroll through it by yourself. If you like what you see, agree to meet up. If you don't, politely decline and move on. See how uneventful that is? That's what you want until you find someone worth talking about.

You might be wondering how you can make a decision about a new love interest without at least *some* feedback from your trusted confidants. My guess is that you're feeling this way because you don't trust yourself or your gut. Maybe you've been wrong before. Maybe you've been hurt before. And maybe you have a diagnosed disorder that makes you question every little thing you do. My hope is that through the prompts and suggestions in this book, you now have a pretty clear idea of what type of partner you are looking for and how to find out if someone matches that criteria. But if you're looking for another way to help determine if you've met someone worth pursuing, I have a suggestion. While I like to call it my patented three-tier system, it's basically just three questions to ask yourself to gauge whether you're settling. Also, it's absolutely not patented. Without further ado:

Test One: The Bar
Is the person above or below your "bar" when it comes to physical attraction? Above = physically attractive to you. Below = not physically attractive to you. For me, I know if someone is above or below my bar upon seeing them with my eyes for the first time. For others, it might change over time, like we talked about earlier. Keep in mind everyone's bar is vastly different, and it has to do with personal preference, not traditional beauty standards.

Test Two: The Mall
Would you be proud to walk around a mall with this person? Are they someone you want to show off? This isn't about physical appearance—it's about how you view them as a whole. If you ran

into an old colleague, would you be embarrassed to introduce them to your new sweetheart, or would you be pumped?

Test Three: Family Dinner
Would this person fit in nicely if you invited them to have dinner with your family? And I'm not exclusively talking about blood relatives. I'm talking about the people you love most in your life. Do you see this person getting along with your nearest or dearest, or would there be obvious conflict and/or lack of connection?

If these tests seem over the top or silly because no one goes to malls anymore, let me simplify it even further. When deciding whether to move forward with someone, there is one key question you must ask yourself: Do you respect them? Not just do you respect their opinions or their basic rights as a human being, but do you respect how they live their life? Do you respect how they spend their time? Do you respect how they conduct themselves in the world? Every time I've initiated a breakup with a boyfriend, it was because, in addition to all the surface-level problems, I didn't respect them deep down. This doomed our relationship from the start, regardless of how much chemistry and fun we had. For example, one of my exes spent a lot of time volunteering for his old film fraternity, so much so that he held a high position within the organization. While many people might consider this admirable or cool, I personally found it to be a waste of time that would have been better spent pursuing his actual career goals. As a result, I didn't respect his judgment or interests, and this tarnished my overall opinion of him. Meanwhile, I'm sure he could sense that I didn't respect this huge part of his life, which couldn't have been a great feeling.

Again, this all ties back to individual compatibility and self-awareness. When your potential partner shares their favorite hobby with you, ask yourself if you respect the hobby or if you find it silly. When they share their dreams and aspirations, do you believe they have what it takes to achieve them or do you find them delusional? Basically, if they were a company, would you invest your own money in them? I know this might sound harsh, but if everyone was compatible with everyone, you wouldn't be

"It's okay to have preferences and opinions. You are allowed to be selective without implying you're better than other people."

reading this book in the first place. You'd be too busy attending multiple weddings every weekend. It's okay to have preferences and opinions. You are allowed to be selective without implying you're better than other people. One person's pass might be your future spouse and vice versa. Pretty much every amazing person in the world has been dumped at least once. I think about that often and it brings me much comfort!

Before we head into our FINAL CHAPTER, I want to mention one more option when it comes to dating: using a matchmaking service. These services might be worth exploring if you feel like you simply don't have enough time to date around or if you want to add another avenue for meeting people. Unfortunately, match-making services are often prohibitively expensive, but there is a fun loophole. Any big matchmaking company, including the one Devyn works for, always has a pool of candidates to set their clients up with. Sometimes it's completely free to join the pool, and other times you have to pay a yearly fee. Do a little research and see if there are some companies in your area that are worth joining! A large part of being open to dating is simply being open, whether that's online, in real life, or through a matchmaker (professional or amateur). I successfully set up two of my friends simply because they were down to give it a shot (and I am great at matchmaking).

Dating is scary. Dating is fun. Dating is exhausting. Dating is exhilarating. Dating is often something you simply have to do if you want to find a romantic partner. While I can't provide you with step-by-step instructions to ensure that you find the love of your life in thirty days or less, I hope you feel more prepared to take on the challenge than you did before. You're not going into this process ill-equipped or uninformed. You now know how to set yourself up for success and the least amount of heartache. And you know how to avoid wasting anyone's time. Be open. Be honest. And write the following bullet points on your bathroom mirror so you don't forget them:

- Make sure the photos on your dating profile accurately portray your lifestyle.

- When dating online, try to have fun and be your authentic self. This encourages the other person to do the same. It also helps you determine if you're actually a good match.

- Disclose your intentions and boundaries before things turn physical.

- Dating multiple people at once might help alleviate your anxiety and prevent you from putting too much pressure on one relationship.

- Figure out the vision you have for your life and find out the vision your potential partner has for theirs. If they don't align, move on!

- Do not ghost! Instead, be compassionately direct. (And if someone ghosts you, assume they have been abducted by friendly aliens.)

- Be open to meeting people in many different ways.

- Make time for self-care.

- Not talking as much about your dating life might make it easier to not obsess as much about your dating life.

- Remember, you are looking for the VP of your life! It's okay to have a lot of job requirements.

Penultimate is one of my favorite words, and we have somehow reached the end of the penultimate chapter. Please keep reading! There's more! And it's juicy!

CHAPTER EIGHT

HOW DO I NOT GIVE UP?

When I first conceived of the idea for this book, I had just started dating someone new. I will call him Ben. When my agent started sending out my book proposal to potential publishers, Ben and I were visiting New York so he could meet my entire family and see my hometown. When I found out (many months later) that I had actually sold the book, Ben and I were happily living together. And as I tirelessly wrote the first draft of this book, my left hand sparkled against the keyboard, because Ben and I were ENGAGED. All of my dreams had come true. After years of heartache, I had finally met my person and we were building a life together. I spent entire showers fantasizing about going on my book tour, newly married and confident—both in my work and in my love life. I was a success story! I was living proof that everything in this book actually works! It was going to be a number one bestseller, and I would probably get a TV show out of it!

And then he left me. And my life imploded. The end.

Just kidding! Except about him leaving me. That really did happen, and it was shocking and traumatic and unbelievably painful. I've debated both with myself and others about how much of this "breakup" I should disclose here. I put "breakup" in quotes because to me, it didn't feel like a breakup. It felt like an abandonment. I had no choice in the decision, nor did I see it coming. The rug was ripped out from under me during a pandemic, and as I sobbed uncontrollably, no one was able to come to my apartment to comfort me because it wasn't safe to be indoors with someone who wasn't already in your bubble. And my bubble had just burst. Leaving me alone. Again. It was my greatest fear realized.

And guess what? It fucking sucked. And it still sucks. I would never wish this experience on anyone (except maybe that one girl who bullied me at summer camp). The pain of this experience was multidimensional. In addition to having to deal with all the regular grief that comes with having your heart ripped out of your chest, my sense of reality was turned upside down because I did not previously believe Ben was capable of doing this to me. In my mind, "engaged" was the same as "married" (minus a piece of paper and an overpriced party). While I knew things had been off, I attributed the change to his mental health and, I don't know, the fact that we were experiencing a *pandemic*. It was a rough patch, sure, but I thought we would get through it together. I never imagined that on one random Monday night, I would find out he was completely done with the relationship, had no interest in working on it at all, and was ready and willing to never see me again. Within an hour of this shocking disclosure, Ben had my engagement ring in his pocket, a backpack filled with some essentials, and a firm determination that his life would be better without me, because "something was missing." I called my parents sobbing on the bathroom floor as he finished gathering his stuff. It felt surreal, unbearable, and overwhelmingly unfair. He was my PERSON. How could he just leave me?!? How could he not even give us an opportunity to try to fix things?! Surely, in the clarity of morning, he would realize he owed it to me—owed it to us—to at least try to work through his doubts and the fact that he "wasn't excited about the future." We were a partnership. Our parents had vacationed together. We had a wedding date. You don't just LEAVE.

But that's exactly what he did. And aside from two brief phone calls and an emotionless email, I have not seen or spoken to him since. During our last phone conversation, a few days after he left, Ben repeatedly declared that it was better for me if I didn't harbor any "false hope." Also, when could he come get his stuff so he could start to move forward with his life? I felt like I was talking to a stranger. Every point I made—*maybe this is your anxiety, maybe we can work on this, maybe you're not excited about the future because we are in the middle of civil unrest as a mysterious disease ravages the world and destroys society as we know it*—was met with eerily calm objections. Apparently, he had already considered all these things on his own time and determined them not to be true. I just hadn't had the privilege of being included in that process. Instead, I was told the decision was made and it was time for me to accept my new reality. Even though it felt much more like *The Twilight Zone* than real life.

Ben moved all his stuff out once I was far away in New York, where I had gone to be with my family. He was supposed to let me know after he'd dropped his keys off with my friend, but he didn't. He had no interest in checking in on me or making sure that I was able to get to the airport safely despite being in a state of extreme shock. After all, as he explained calmly during one of those brief calls, this decision "wasn't abrupt for him." Apparently, he had been having doubts for months, so he had to listen to his gut and do what he now knew, without a doubt, was absolutely right. I have to say, this was uncharacteristic clarity for someone who was historically indecisive. But he was done. And we were over.

I'm not sharing these details with you to bash Ben or portray him as an undeniably bad person. (I have plenty of theories about what led him to the decisions he made, and while I don't agree with them, I understand how he got to a place where he felt he had to completely disconnect from me in order to be happy—or at least have the potential for future happiness.) I'm sharing these details with you so you know that what happened to me was my absolute worst-case scenario. Every fear I have ever had came to fruition:

- I was left.

- I was left without warning.

- We were ENGAGED and everyone knew and he still left.

- The reason for him leaving revolved around him NOT LOVING ME ENOUGH.

- He was able to walk away from me without a single glance back.

- He did not appear to miss me or regret his decision at all.

- His entire family immediately cut ties and never contacted me again.

- I suddenly became single and I fucking hate being single.

- He chose to handle things in the cruelest way possible, leading me to believe I meant nothing to him.

- He didn't even care enough to try.

- I still loved him, but he was gone.

It was quite literally the stuff of my (recurring) nightmares. And yet, here I am, still standing.

When Dylan dumped me in April 2017, my mind instantly went to death. The pain was so intense that I no longer wanted to live. I did not see any reason to keep going and I was convinced that the rest of my life would be pure misery. The only reason I didn't attempt suicide was out of courtesy to my family. (Plus, my mom immediately flew out to LA just in case.) I remember wailing over and over again, "I am not okay. I am not okay." When I was abandoned in November 2020, the pain was excruciating and the situation was objectively worse. This time I wasn't being left by my boyfriend of ten months who lived in an adult version of a frat house. I was being left by my *fiancé*, whom I had already been living with for over a year. A man who, as part of my proposal scavenger hunt, had officially adopted my dog as his own. A man who I was planning on dedicating this very book to: "To Ben, my happy ending." (Yeah, right!) And yet, despite all of this, I did not want to die. I knew immediately that I would be okay. I wasn't sure if I would be happy again, but I knew I would be okay.

If this abandonment had happened at an earlier time in my life, it might have broken me. I did not have the self-love or coping skills to deal with this level of grief and rejection. I would have immediately internalized the situation and decided that I was the problem. I was unlovable. I was worthless. I would not have been able to sit with that level of emotional discomfort without turning to suicidal ideation and self-harm. I would not have been able to get myself to New York with my dog and an abundance of disposable face masks only four days later. (To be fair, I did not do these things alone. My parents booked my flight and sent me the masks, but I was in good enough shape to let them.) I knew I needed to go home to heal, so I did what I had to do to make that happen. As I stood in the airport, waiting for my flight and standing at least six feet away from everyone else, the small part of me that wasn't numb marveled at my own strength. I felt like a badass. A wounded, heartbroken badass. But a badass, nonetheless.

There is already an entire chapter in this book about breakups, so I don't want to indulgently reiterate what you've already read, but I would like to point out a few key factors that have really helped my healing process. The first is my increased self-worth. About a month before Ben left, we had a tough discussion that I thought was a sign of us being able to effectively communicate. (Unfortunately, it's pretty impossible to effectively communicate if your partner is only telling you 70 percent of their truth and you don't have all the information.) I knew he hadn't been feeling like himself and had some concerns about me and our future. (This is totally normal, by the way, and not a clear sign that your partner is going to walk out on you four weeks later.) If anything, part of the shock came from the fact that I thought we *were* really good at communicating, even when it was uncomfortable and hard. But again, I wasn't working with all of the information, like the extent of his doubts or his internal debate over whether or not to walk away. To me, walking away wasn't even on the table, given our recent engagement and commitment to each other. Plus, I had asked him many times if our relationship was the main source of his recent unease and had been assured that was not the case. Looking back, he clearly didn't want to hurt me by admitting his true feelings, but by doing so, he completely cut me out of the decision-making process. Yet another reminder to fill your partner in on what you're mentally going through so as not to completely blindside them later.

Anyway! As he was expressing these potential issues, including a fear that I would make him leave Southern California (something I had assured him *many* times I would not do), I distinctly remember sitting there thinking, *It's so weird he's being like this, because I am pretty awesome.* I know this might sound like a strange thought, but over the past few years I have come to not only love myself, but truly *like* myself. And as a result of this, I didn't internalize his concerns about me. I had enough self-awareness to see that his "idea" of me was blurred and inaccurate. He often worried I was going to force him to do something he didn't want to do, even though that is not in my nature. If anything, I am too accommodating. (Something that's now on my list of things to work through.) So while I was hurt and pissed off during that conversation— especially since my grandma had died earlier *that very day*—the one thing I didn't do was shit on myself. Instead, I listened to his concerns, promised to work on a few things that I could control, and calmly asked him to show me more affection. And in the weeks that followed, he did, which made me feel better.

The irony here is that after years of being anxiously attached, I had finally become so securely attached that I didn't think our relationship was the problem. Instead of demanding constant reassurance, I gave him space and tried to be there for him as he applied for a new job. (He left me on his first day of said job.) I felt a bit unloved and underappreciated, but instead of spiraling out of control over it, I thought it would pass once he was in a better place.

A part of me was still angry at him for aspects of that earlier conversation (and for not letting us adopt a foster dog I had become extremely attached to), but I knew those feelings would eventually pass. It was a pandemic! It was 2020! It was okay to feel a bit off for a while! I was so confident in myself that I couldn't see how insecure he was about us.

Looking back, I've wondered if feeling so secure was a mistake. If I had been more worried, would I have been able to fix things before he completely disconnected from me, blew up our lives, and ran away? But the answer is . . . it's not one person's job to save or fix a relationship. If he had come to me, told me about his concern that "something was missing," and asked if we could try to work through it together, I know I would have done that. I would have tried couples therapy. I would have geared myself up for more tough conversations. Would it have saved us? Maybe, maybe not. But I know I would have at least tried. He just never gave me that opportunity. So here's a big takeaway from my experience: You can't regret not taking opportunities that you weren't given. I could sit in my brain all day and think about what I can now recognize as warning signs and try to imagine different reactions that might have led to a different outcome. But not only would this be a waste of time, it would also be damaging to my psyche. What-if thoughts are mental poison, and I have already been hurt enough. I want to be my protector, not my enemy. So I did what I could to veer away from that dangerous rabbit hole.

Avoiding said rabbit hole did not come easily. It's human nature to feel like you are the main character of every story. You are with yourself 24/7! Your perspective of the world is filtered through how different experiences affect *you*. So when someone rejects you, it feels like that decision is completely tied up in who you are as a person. But sometimes it actually doesn't have to do with you: it has to do with them and their journey. Maybe they weren't ready. Maybe they have unrealistic expectations about long-term relationships. Maybe they truly think you are great but simply don't want the same life that you want. Maybe you will never truly know what the fuck happened, but you can rest assured that you will never treat someone the way you have been treated. There is power in knowing you are not going to change your morals in reaction to pain.

Following my abandonment, many people said something to the effect of "maybe you needed this experience to learn something" in an effort to console me. And I have to be honest: That response really pissed me off, because I *was* and *am* ready for marriage. I didn't need someone to break my heart (again) in order to truly find and value myself. That part of my growth had already happened. But then my therapist said, "You might not have needed this life lesson, but maybe he did," and I felt something shift inside me. It had been harmful to view my abandonment as something that was happening *to* me instead of something that was just happening. In this instance, maybe I wasn't the main character at all, but someone who had to get killed off for the protagonist to accomplish his mission. Maybe he'll never accomplish it. But I know there is no point in checking his social media to find out. I have to return to my own story and forge ahead without him.

It's helped me to remember that a reality of life is that it doesn't always go the way you want it to. Many things are out of our control. Sometimes that means you get in a car accident. Sometimes that means your fiancé leaves even though you really want them to stay. Neither incident directly correlates with your value as a person. You are just one piece in a huge factory of moving parts. Every now and then you are going to get knocked over. You can't avoid that. All you can do is work on improving your recovery time and your resilience so the next blow doesn't hurt as much. One way to help with this is to build a great support system.

In the months leading up to my world being turned upside down, I felt disconnected from many people in my life. This was understandable given the pandemic, but it was an issue I had been dealing with on and off before 2020. I felt like my friends didn't care about or value me that much, and I struggled with the fact that my sister didn't always have time to call me back. I had lost multiple close friendships in 2019 and was extra sensitive in that area. I even felt resentment toward my dog because she appeared to prefer Ben and wasn't showing me the type of overbearing affection one expects from a dog. So while I finally had a fiancé, I felt that the rest of my support system, apart from my parents, was vulnerable. And then two surprising things happened.

The first, as you know, was Ben leaving me on a random Monday night around 9:30 p.m. And the second was the unbelievable outpouring of support from the very people I thought didn't care that much. The day after he left, three different friends sent me food, including a pineapple and olive pizza. (Sounds gross, but it is actually not that gross.) In the weeks that followed, my sister checked in on me and talked to me more than in the past two years combined. People I hadn't spoken to in a long time sent me incredible messages about how much they value me and shared stories from their own lives to help me feel less alone. As soon as I arrived in New York, my dog was more affectionate than she has ever been in all the years I've had her. (She might have just been thrilled to suddenly have access to a backyard, but either way, I'll take it.) While my heart had rapidly lost the love of the person I valued most in the world, everyone else was stepping in to fill it back up. I might not have needed a lesson when it came to romantic relationships, but this experience did prove, without a doubt, the importance of having a support system outside of my partnership. My life wasn't over because Ben was never my whole life.

Throughout this book, I have harped on the importance of "doing the work." I've waxed poetic about the need to be stable enough on your own before you enter into a relationship. I

> "I deserve to share all of this love I hold inside myself with another person."

believed all of those things when I first wrote them, but I was writing them from a place of privilege with an engagement ring on my finger and a handsome man in the next room. There was a part in the first draft of this book where I said something to the effect of "I know that if my relationship ever ended, I would still be okay." And when I wrote those words, there was a small part of me that wondered, *Is that really true? Or does that just fit the narrative I am pushing?* Now, as much as I wish this wasn't the case, I know the answer. My relationship ended, and I *am* okay. I've had bad moments and harmful thoughts, but I never fell all the way down. I had set up too many safety nets ahead of time to catch me. I used to think that I was a success story because, despite years of failed relationships and mental health struggles, I had finally found a life partner. Now I *know* I am a success story because the person who I believed was my life partner left me, I survived it, and I haven't given up on love or myself.

There is a version of this story where my takeaway would be to no longer trust other people. I would build walls around my heart and give up on the partnership I've always wanted because the thought of being hurt this deeply again is too much to bear. That would be the easy route. But I deserve more than that. I deserve to find a partner who won't walk away when things get a little tough. I deserve to share all of this love I hold inside myself with another person. I deserve to have a family that I will support as fiercely as my family has supported me. So instead of learning to distrust other people, this experience has shown me that I can always trust myself. No matter what happens, my life is in good hands. They just happen to be my own.

"No matter what happens, my life is in good hands. They just happen to be my own."

In the introduction to this book, I promised all of you that there wouldn't be a twist ending. I wouldn't suddenly shift from focusing on romantic love to making a declaration that self-love is all you need. And while my personal life did have a twist I definitely didn't see coming, I stand by my promise. In my weakest moments since Ben left, I've worried that I won't find love again. I've agonized over the possibility that I will never find someone as compatible or wonderful. I've panicked that all the "good ones" will be taken. I've wondered if maybe I should just resign myself to a life of singlehood and yummy meals for one. But then my sister said, "If you prioritize finding a partner, you will find a partner. You just have to"—say it with me now—"put in the work." And I know she is right. So, I am going to put my money where my mouth is and do what I need to do to find a life partner. I'm going to put myself out there while not reverting to an anxious attachment style and waiting for my phone to ring. And once I find my life partner, I am going to use all of the tools we've talked about to nurture the relationship and make sure it is healthy for both of us. It probably won't be smooth sailing, but hey, I've already been through (and survived) worse. My metaphorical ship is built to last in the toughest of conditions. Plus, I can always refer back to my own words when I need a confidence boost. Turns out, I wrote this book in the nick of time.

You're not going to believe it, but we've somehow come to the end of this journey. I hope after reading all this you have a better understanding of what you want in a romantic relationship and the best practices for finding and maintaining a healthy one. I hope you filled at least some of that notebook I made you buy. And I hope, above all else, that you remain hopeful. Your life partner is out there, and they will be so thankful for all the hard work you've done to set your relationship up for success. I know I am, and I'm not even dating you! I guess if I *had* to summarize everything we've learned together, it boils down to this:

- Don't give up on yourself, and don't give up on love.

I pinky promise to do the same.

Acknowledgments

I want to start off by thanking my incredible support system. I could not have finished this book and gotten through my broken engagement without all of you. While I was consumed with sobs and shame, you gently told me the book would be better off with the inclusion of my recent heartbreak, and I trusted you enough to believe you. I now know you were right.

Thank you to my manager, Matt Sadeghian. Every career success I have can be traced back to you, your cunning mind, and your unwavering support.

Thank you to Brianne Johnson for helping me sell this thing and for guiding me through the (sometimes) harrowing process.

Thank you to Writers House and my agent, Stacy Testa. Even though you joined this project in the middle, your support has been resolute and much appreciated.

Thank you to my team at Workman Publishing and my editor, Rachael Mt. Pleasant. You understood what I wanted to accomplish from our first conversation and helped me get there with a guiding hand and instrumental insight.

Thank you to Dr. Carrie Castañeda-Sound for your thoughtful consultation on the Note to the Reader.

A HUGE thank you to everyone I interviewed for this project! Robin Gibbs, Joanna Robin, Sheva Rajaee, Annette Rotter, Zac Seidler, Jennifer Yashari, Jessica O'Reilly, Devyn Simone, and Nick Notas: Your expertise is what made this project so valuable. And thank you to those who gave their time and hearts but remained anonymous. Sharing our stories is one of the greatest gifts we can give.

A special thank you to my family. This was a scary and vulnerable thing to do. I could not have done it without knowing I had your full support behind me! (Just don't read chapter six.)

And to everyone who has ever thought they were unlovable. This one's for you.